VIKING
WARFARE

VIKING WARFARE

I. P. STEPHENSON

AMBERLEY

Dedicated to Nicki, Corin & Andrew

First published 2012

Amberley Publishing
The Hill, Stroud
Gloucestershire, GL5 4EP

www.amberley-books.com

British Library Cataloguing in Publication Data.
A catalogue record for this book is available from the British Library.

ISBN 978 1 84868 690 8

Typeset in 10pt on 12pt Sabon.
Typesetting and Origination by Amberley Publishing.
Printed in the UK.

Contents

Preface and Acknowledgements   7

1. *Víkingr!*   11

2. 'Lies, Damn Lies and Sagas'   19

3. The Wrath of God   25

4. Bright Wargear   39

5. 'Hold Their Shields Aright'   77

6. The Place of Slaughter   93

Bibliography   115

Index   123

Preface and Acknowledgements

Viking is such a vivid word, steeped in imagery and blood. Thus a book on the subject of Viking warfare should, I suppose, start with images of battle, probably drawn from one of the many survivor Sagas. Egil's maybe, with its description of the Battle of Brunanburgh fought in AD 937, a great defeat for the Vikings and their allies, but spectacularly brought to life (or is it?) in the *Saga of Egil Skallagrimsson*, or possibly we should turn to one of the legends? To the Volsungs, or *Hrolfs Saga Kraka*, or to the Edda (poetic and prose)?

We will look at and deal with the Sagas, the Edda and of course the Battle of Brunanburgh, as well of course as the Battle of Maldon, but not yet and not straightaway. In many ways the Vikings and their age are a question of perception, and this point will be dealt with in greater detail in the first chapter. However, before we get there some ancient history, or should that be early medieval history?

Growing up in Jarrow in the North East of England, the Vikings were to some extent always present, albeit at a generally prosaic level. Jarrow is the site of the monastery of St Paul, part of the twin monastery of Wearmouth-Jarrow. St Peter's on the River Wear was founded in AD 674 by Benedict Biscop. The more famous St Paul's on the River Tyne was founded in AD 681. It was granted to the Church by King Ecgfrith of Northumbria. The *more famous* because it was at the younger foundation that the Venerable Bede both lived and worked – Jarrow on the banks of the Tyne is the birthplace of English history for here, 'Herodotus like', Bede penned what we view as his masterwork, the *Historia Ecclesiastica Gentis Anglorum*. Primarily a Church history, it remains none the less one of the foundation texts of the Anglo-Saxon period.

Yet as a child this was but background, for the planners and architects of Jarrow, in conceiving a monstrosity of a shopping centre, turned to the events of AD 794 as recorded in Simeon of Durham's twelfth-century *History of Kings of England*, and the purported sack of the monastery by the Vikings became their inspiration. Thus they created the Viking Centre with its great, crude statue of two Vikings suitably horned-helmeted looking towards the river. They looked to the river and I stared at them every time I went with my father to the bank.

My only other real brush with the Vikings as a child, apart from the odd visit to Lindisfarne, were stories told by my maternal grandfather of Viking longships sailing up the stream at the back of his house, which he assured me was far wider and deeper in the past, attacking all the nearby villages. I now tell my daughter similar suitably tall tales, not yet about the Vikings, but they will probably come. Although she does love *Noggin the Nog* and knows all the stories.

Growing up in the North East, York also featured in my childhood, but *Yorvik* was simply a tourist novelty, and there were other more interesting things to see.

University changed all of that. As an undergraduate at Newcastle I discovered a passion for Anglo-Saxon history, concentrating on that in preference to what I saw as the rather dull subject that I had gone there to read. Post-graduate studies again at Newcastle, this time actually on an aspect of early Anglo-Saxon warfare, further deepened my interest in the period, which despite subsequent research in other areas and periods, has never gone away.

You cannot study Anglo-Saxon warfare without looking at the Vikings; they are the other side of the hill so to speak. They are the 'ten-foot high' bogeymen who almost snuffed out the Anglo-Saxon kingdoms, and in the process acted as the catalyst in the creation of Bede's great dream, made real by Alfred of Wessex and his heirs – namely England. On top of this the Vikings, or so it is at times argued (and we will look at this in more detail later and, generally throughout the book), were different, they operated outside of contemporary customs and norms – but was this so? Or were they just more successful than their contemporaries?

The Vikings today are different things to different people, and although in this work we are concerned with the Vikings at war, we must, however, before we begin to address the subject of Viking warfare consider the meaning of the word. Nomenclature is followed by an examination of the evidence, both primary and secondary, and then and only then do we get to the meat of the matter.

As an Anglo-Saxonist it is nice to be standing on the other side of the hill for a change. Peter Kemmis Betty and Alan Sutton as ever deserve many thanks and I cannot thank them enough for allowing me to do this, as well as all the support (and patience) over the years.

It goes, not quite without saying, that two extraordinary people, Lindsay Allason-Jones and Heinrich Härke deserve a great deal of thanks for helping to shape my thought processes over the years; as a result my voyage has been everywhere and my intent everything.

Friends and family have as ever been playing their part and my thanks are due to Dr Zarqa Khawaja; without her this seemed as if it would never see the light of day – never was the bright coffee better bought! Fiona Mayes, Paul Mullis (who like me was more interested in the Anglo-Saxon than in his own undergraduate studies), Alex Croom, Bill and Karen Griffiths, Marcus Davies, Jon and Carola Attwater, the latter particularly for a marvellous conversation we had years ago about Georgette Heyer and the Vikings (a subject which we will obliquely touch upon later). Miriam Daniels has as ever provided some superb illustrations. I am also very grateful to Katie Clegg for her keyboard skills.

Finally my thanks and love go to my parents and of course my daughter Isabella for all of their help support, and in Isabella's case, distractions.

Ian Stephenson
Reading 2011

1

Víkingr!

'From the Halls of Montezuma to the shores of Tripoli' – so the song of the US Marine Corps goes. A bit of an odd place to start for a book on the Vikings, but these ten words nicely help to begin to delineate the problem faced by anyone looking at the Vikings and the Viking age, and that is before we even get on to the subject of what exactly we mean by the word 'Viking'.

The Vikings were great traders, explorers (for profit), sailors, settlers and above all warriors. They were the first Europeans to settle in the North American continent, they travelled the great rivers of continental Russia from the Baltic to the Black Sea, visiting the lands of the Mediterranean via both the Dardanelles and the Straits of Gibraltar, as well as their more obvious exploits in the islands of Britain and against the Franks. As Rus they fought the people of the steppes and the Byzantine Empire, in the process helping to found the kingdom of Russia. As Varangians they are remembered as the most loyal and most famous of the Byzantine Empire's mercenary troops. In Spain and along the coast of North Africa they attacked the Caliphate of Cordoba and the Abbasid Caliphate. While on the other side of the Atlantic they faced hostility and competition for resources from Inuit and Native American tribes. In the British Isles they settled and created kingdoms on the islands of Faeroe, Shetland, Orkney and the Hebrides as well as in the north of Scotland and Ireland. In England they came very close to completely snuffing out the great kingdoms of the Anglo-Saxon heptarchy. Under Cnut they carved out a great Scandinavian Empire with England as its centre. They besieged London, Paris and Constantinople. Sacking monasteries, they sent the body at St Cuthbert on a great travelling odyssey. They fought among themselves, suffered staggeringly spectacular defeats and in their turn won great victories – both of which inspired wonderful soaring heroic poetry. Finally and fatefully for this country, fighting Carolingians and Ottonians they carved out the Duchy of Normandy in northern France. All of this in the space of less than three hundred years – the first described attack took place in AD 789, the last in AD 1013 or AD 1066 or AD 1070, depending on how you choose to date it.

In this list of places visited, pillaged and sacked, as well of peoples fought, we begin to approach the problem of Viking warfare. Harald Hardrada, King of

Norway, travelled, so his saga tells us, through Russia; he was a Varangian and fought in the Mediterranean before he reclaimed his ancestors' throne. Harald, as King of Norway, then fought a long and fruitless war against Denmark before dying in battle at Stamford Bridge in the north of England. He was viewed, according to William of Poitiers, as 'the most valiant warrior under Heaven'. Yet he was hardly typical. Then again, in military terms was there such a thing as a typical Viking, or do we see a range of similar behaviour and experience confined to separate areas? Thus Vikings in England had one set of experiences, which were quite similar to the experience of those Vikings who operated in Ireland, Scotland and the Carolingian world, but were different to Vikings in Greenland and North America. Equally, the Rus, Byzantium and Mediterranean worlds, which all to some extent overlapped, provided the Vikings with a different set of experiences.

These areas, these spheres, all interconnected to some extent with each other. People, goods, fashions and ideas will all to some degree have travelled between them. Thus at Birka, situated on the island of Björkö in Lake Mälar, famously Sweden's largest Viking Age town, we find steppe-style belts and belt mounts worn as status objects by the town's warrior garrison. Sweden had by this point in its history had a long relationship with East Anglia, see for example the Sutton Hoo finds, and in this context we see the potential for a degree of steppe style to cross the North Sea to England. However, given the lack of similar finds in this country we should view it more as an individual or small group affectation, as opposed to a more universal Viking style. Equally, staying with Eastern fashion, the use of the mace in warfare had been a factor in Romano-Persian and steppe combat, particularly mounted combat, from before the Viking age. Yet for all this and despite the weapon's obvious usefulness, particularly against an armoured opponent, it was never universally adopted by either the Romans or the Sassanid Persians. Nor other than by association can we connect the mace with the Rus, although they are more likely to have been used by Vikings in Russia than anywhere else. However, as with the Birka belt fittings, we cannot rule out individual taste.

To compound this, if we turn to the far west we see the Vikings fighting Inuit and Native Americans. These people had a completely different style and method of warfare to the European Greco-Roman tradition of warfare practiced by the Vikings. None of this points to homogeneity, nor given the geographical spread should we expect it to. Therefore, if we plan to write about Viking warfare we should, so to speak, pick our battlefield. In order to do this the main determinant is evidence. Thus we turn to England.

England immediately prior to the Viking Age consisted of a series of well ordered, if not always peaceful, Christian polities. They were literate, which the Vikings at this time were not, or at least not in a way that is useful to us. Thus Anglo-Saxon England provides us with a series of contemporary writing: poems, annals, chronicles and lives, to name some of the more obvious sources which greatly help to illuminate our understanding of this period. Coupled with this, we have a wealth of archaeological and representational evidence, all of which helps to ensure that our understanding of Viking warfare is better, or at least more comprehensive, for England than possibly anywhere else in the Viking world. This is by no means to say it is complete, for when we look at the evidence in more detail we find that we must draw in other pieces of evidence from elsewhere within the Viking world as a whole in order to help complete the picture.

Before looking at what we are going to cover in this work, the question must be answered as to what exactly we mean by the term 'Viking'? A name does more than define a thing: it creates an image, a perception. Most of the time the words are simply prosaic, as indeed are the images they conjure up. This cannot be said of the word 'Viking'. No, here we have layers of complexity. However, the image created depends very much on one's own perspective. The origin of the word, despite much debate and discussion, is uncertain. By the late Viking age it had come in West Norse to mean either a pirate or raider – *Víkingr*. Alternatively, it meant warfare or more simply harrying, specifically at or from the sea – *viking*. Today the word means so much more than this, for over time it has accrued additional meanings.

Of course, that meaning will depend on cultural background, and given that this book is primarily concerned with the Vikings and the English, we will attempt to answer the question of meaning from an English viewpoint. Therefore when we talk about the Vikings, the Viking period, the Viking world, what exactly do we mean? Is there a single simple definition that fits all and neatly describes our discussion? The answer is of course no. Firstly because we are not dealing with a static phenomenon, and secondly because we are dealing with perceptions of the past. Different groups and individuals project their own priorities and preconceptions on to the subject. Thus the Vikings and the Viking age will be defined in one way by the general public, which may differ from the academic view of the Viking age. Before looking at either viewpoint we must, however, go back and look at the development of such views.

At times the primary purpose of history has been legitimisation. We do such a thing, or such a person is in charge because of, and here we insert the historical justification. In terms of kings and rulers, legitimisation or throne-worthiness came from having the correct ancestry. Thus in Anglo-Saxon England we see the great dynasties tracing their ancestry back primarily to Wodin (the Norse Odin). The East Saxons, unusually, traced their descent from the god Seaxnet. Christianity barely impacted upon this. After the conversion Woden simply became a part of the regnal list which now stretched back in direct lines to Adam, his (Woden's) role as a successful war-god being supplanted by a more powerful but equally martial alternative – namely the Christian God.

Snorri Sturluson's early thirteenth-century work *Heimskringla* or *History of the Kings of Norway* performed a similar function, albeit without the bolted-on Christianity, to the Anglo-Saxon regnal lists. The kings of Norway, according to Snorri, could trace their lineage, through the kings, battles and harryings, to a (mythical) great warrior king Óthin, or as he is more commonly known, the god Odin.

Culturally, the Anglo-Saxons shared a very similar present and past with the Scandinavian world. The change came with the end of the Anglo-Saxon age. The year AD 1066 saw the end of Anglo-Saxon England; it has also been seen as the end of the Viking age. But the Vikings at the end of the Viking age were not the same as at the beginning, for in many ways the Viking age in England ended in 1013 with the invasion of Swein Forkbeard.

The Norman Conquest reset the historical clock. William the Conqueror, as he now was, traced his claim to the throne through his cousin, the late King Edward. William's heirs and successors saw no need to base their legitimacy on belonging to either the House of Cerdic or to the defeated Anglo-Danish line of Swein and Cnut. Anglo-Saxon England faded into the background. Henry VIII resurrected it slightly, during his 'great matter' (his divorce from Catherine of Aragon) and his dispute with the papacy, citing the 'ancient rights' of the English (Anglo-Saxon) Church in support of his argument. But it was his during the reign of his daughter, Elizabeth, that we see the rise of the antiquarian scholar and an increasing interest in pre-conquest England, particularly in Asser's life of Alfred. His rise as a great king dates back to this period and you cannot have Alfred without the Vikings. The Georgian and Victorian periods saw Alfred the Great lauded as the founder of the Royal Navy. Further strengthening this resurgence of interest in the Viking period were the great ship finds of Oseberg and Gokstad.

Millais' 1843 pen and ink drawing 'The Danes Committing Barbarous Ravages over the Coast of England' epitomises what is still considered by many to be the archetypal image of the Danes or Vikings – that of the savage pirate. This image, popularised in books and films up to the present day, is not only surprisingly enduring but has also survived the academic onslaught of the late twentieth century.

Paul B. De Chaillu's two-volume 1889 work *The Viking Age* is absolutely wonderful; the books themselves, although concentrating on all aspects of society, do cover the subject of warfare in far more detail than anything else. Matters had not changed substantially by 1937, the year of publication of Shetelig and Falk's *Scandinavian Archaeology*. The chapter on the Viking age interweaves the raider and martial aspects of the age with its archaeology; equally the chapter on weapons concentrates on those of the Viking period.

However, an increasing growth in our archaeological knowledge coupled with an empire coping with the after effects of two world wars in less than half a century has tended to make Viking warfare academically unfashionable. Instead, we have seen other aspects of Scandinavian society come to the fore.

Excavated in 1880, the Gokstad ship is the classic Viking warship; found with thirty-two shields in situ on each side of the vessel, it more than any other find encapsulates the raiding ethos we so associate with the Scandinavians of this age. Yet the boat found within the sepulchral chamber, along with the equally spectacular Oseberg ship, points to other aspects of Scandinavian Viking society. Finds, particularly from Oseberg, such as the tent, sleigh, carts, in effect the more mundane everyday non-military artefacts, and not just from the great ship burials but from cemeteries and settlements across the Viking world, have allowed historians and archaeologists to stress the more peaceful side of the Vikings. Thus we are presented with a picture of the Vikings as ship builders, seafarers, traders, explorers, settlers, craftsmen, farmers, lawmakers and artists. But, and this is an important but, a large number of these peaceful activities were either resultant from the activities of, or were designed to support, the ruling warrior elite. Yet for all the academic marginalisation of the Viking warfare, it has not entirely gone away; it usually merits a chapter generally towards the middle or end of most surveys of the period, or in the occasional collections of papers. In the public imagination it has, rightly, not vanished and remains the dominant image of the Vikings. The truth of course was somewhere in between the Tony Curtis, Kirk Douglas 'Vikings' and the stress on Scandinavians in the Viking age as traders and settlers.

The Viking Age in England opens with violence and ended with violence. Separating the three ships in AD 789 and the armies of AD 1066 we see ever-increasing raids, great raiding armies, victories and defeats for both sides, ethnic cleansing, conquest, empire and the merging of cultures. Alongside, of course, trading and settlement. Even if the way wars were fought, the actual mechanics of combat, did not change, the same was not true of the enemy. At times AD 1066 has been advanced as the effective date for the end of the Viking age in England. Why AD 1066? Why not AD 1085 when Cnut of Denmark, according to the Anglo-Saxon Chronicle E manuscript 'set out in this direction, and wanted to win this land'? Part of the reason we choose AD 1066 is that in that year we not only famously see the end of Anglo-Saxon England with the death of Harold II Godwinson in battle at Hastings, but the year also saw the death in battle, at Stamford Bridge just outside of York, of Harald Hardrada of Norway – the greatest warrior of the age, described by some as the last true Viking. However, the state that died as a result of William the Bastard's victory at Hastings was not Anglo-Saxon, it was Anglo-Danish, and in that respect the Viking Age in England ended in AD 1013 with Swein Forkbeard's invasion.

This year, AD 1013, stands as a watershed because it marks a fundamental change in the nature of what we would choose to call Viking warfare, albeit at a strategic level. The world in some respects had changed. Raiding remained a tool, and an effective one at that, and would do for centuries; indeed, in later centuries men such as Drake, Hawkins and Morgan were undoubtedly viewed as 'viking-like' in their behaviour, even if the word itself was never used. However, what we would now increasingly see was the systematic attempt by one sovereign state to conquer another sovereign state. Thus, claiming that the Viking age in England ended in AD 1013 is not as perverse as it may seem. Swein was King of Denmark and acted in that role when seeking to add England to his demesne. He was not some freebooter with a following and the same was true of Harald Hardrada in AD 1066. If anyone came close to the traditional image of the Viking in the events surrounding the fall of Anglo-Danish England, it was William the Bastard. But even here the resemblance is superficial; William, as Duke of Normandy, was the leader of a powerful state and his part-mercenary army was not unusual even in recent English history, Thorkell the Tall having served Æthelred II.

This change was played out in the eleventh century not only in England but in Scandinavia as well, with conflict between Norway and Denmark as sovereign states. The late eleventh/early twelfth century also saw the beginnings of that most un-Viking of activities: crusading, not just in the Holy Land but also in the Baltic, with the good Christian King Eric I of Denmark being the first monarch to visit the new Kingdom of Jerusalem. Thus in the events of AD 1013, where European kingdom warred on European kingdom, we can see the beginnings of the *kabinetskrieg* of later centuries.

What then do we consider in this work? We are looking predominantly at the Vikings in England, but like all things this is both very broad and, specifically in terms of warfare, also potentially very narrow. For in terms of narrowness, if we simply look at the engagements fought then we are in the main looking at a list, a skeleton with very little flesh on the bones.

The first chapter after this introduction, 'Lies, Damn Lies and Sagas', looks at the range and types of evidence available. It thus discusses the archaeological, literary and representational evidence. Archaeology is considered not simply in terms of what is found in this country but takes a broader spread, discussing potential and actual trends as well as influences – both native to Viking and Viking to native. With the literary and representational, we are in the main seeing the Vikings through the eyes of their victims – the reason for this is considered in more detail in the chapter itself. Sagas, the basis of many an introduction to the Vikings, are rarely used here, thus the chapter title, which may possibly be rather harsh on them but, as we will see, only possibly.

Chapter three, 'The Wrath of God', charts the military history of the Viking age in England. The First Viking Age began and ended with Wessex, in that the age opened when three ships arrived at Portland on the Dorset coast, in the kingdom of Wessex. The arrival of these ships precipitated the first English death of the Viking age. The English re-conquest and the triumph of Wessex marked the end of the first Viking age although, as we shall see, the very survival of the English nation (Bede's great dream) did at one point hang in the balance. If the first Viking age was an English triumph, then the second was a time of failure and disaster. Æthelred II was a poor heir of Alfred. English defeat meant, of course, Viking victory – in this case the victor was Cnut, seen by some as the most successful of all Vikings, whose great Scandinavian empire was centred not on his native Denmark but on his 'jewel in the crown' – England. The resultant Anglo-Danish creation, lasting until AD 1066, when the descendant of Vikings – William the Bastard, Duke of Normandy – took advantage of the succession crisis precipitated by the death of Edward the Confessor. Three great battles and the death of two kings are viewed with a certain 'end of the age' inevitability. These were neither the raiders nor the great raiding armies of the first Viking age. Instead, as in AD 1013, we see yet again the forces of one state pitted against another and despite the occasional demonstration by Denmark against England post-AD 1066, the Christian rulers of Scandinavia were turning their thoughts to crusade. The first crusade to the Holy Land took place in AD 1095–99, and a mere four years later King Erik of Denmark was on a pilgrimage to Palestine. The first Northern or Baltic Crusade was launched in AD 1147.

'Bright Wargear' looks at the military equipment of the Vikings: what was available, what was used, why it was adopted and what constituted the minimum level of equipment required for warfare. When looking at why certain pieces of equipment were adopted, the chapter will view it as a two-way process, which indeed it was. Thus the chapter will be primarily a review of Anglo-Viking military equipment, although a broad spectrum of arms and armour from across the whole of the world the Vikings knew will be considered. As a result, we will see the Vikings as both influencers of and influenced by other cultures.

Organisation, army size and tactics are considered in 'Hold Their Shield Aright'. The quote comes from the poem *The Battle of Maldon*, which is itself considered in greater detail in the final chapter. Here, however, we look at how forces were raised, how big they were in relative terms and how they operated on the battlefield. The latter point looks at deployment, command and the mechanics of shield wall combat. The two potentially specialist aspects of the non-heroic archer and the mounted warrior are also considered here, as indeed are the housecarls. Beserkers are not considered here; for reasons which will become readily apparent, they are dealt with in chapter two.

Finally we turn to 'The Place of Slaughter', the Anglo-Saxon Chronicle's evocative phrase for the battlefield. Raiders and their concomitant atrocities are discussed, as of course are naval and siege warfare. In the main, however, the chapter, as its title suggests, concerns itself mainly with the pitch battle. Engagements in this period are not always well documented and we are lucky to have two, Brunanburgh in AD 937 and Maldon in AD 991, about which we talk about in some detail. Other engagements, and of these there is no little number, allow us to use tactical snippets in order to, if not build a complete picture, then to at least cast further light on the subject of Anglo-Viking warfare. The events of AD 1066 and the Anglo-Danish army created by Swein and his son Cnut are of course touched upon; indeed they are difficult to avoid, being as they are such a comparatively rich source of information for the very end of the period.

2
'Lies, Damn Lies and Sagas'

The events of the Battle of Maida in AD 1806 were the foundations upon which Sir Charles Oman built his British line versus French column argument. This, put succinctly, was that in simple mathematical terms the British in line would always beat the French in columns because they could bring more muskets to bear, and as a consequence pour killing volley after killing volley into the French. So much for that theory. In practice, the French at Maida were also in lines and the British system of war relied upon a single volley at close range followed by a bayonet charge. Solid foundations indeed; however, this had not stopped Oman's theory passing into popular imagination. Maida and the Napoleonic Wars may, again, seem an odd place to start, but it illustrates a point, which could equally be made by 'lions led by donkeys' or 'King Arthur', namely that history is replete with myth and legend. As a result, what is accepted as fact is not necessarily so and it is partly in this light that we should view the Viking Sagas.

This is not to say that the Viking Sagas are not a valued source of information, but are they necessarily a source for the Viking age?

This is not as absurd as it may seem; rather it is a serious question. The Sagas have been and continue to be used as evidence for the Vikings. They describe all aspects of life, society and history all across the Viking world, so why should they not be used? They are populated by known historical figures and events and provide detailed description of what we view as major events. Take, for example, the vivid account of the Battle of Brunanburgh in AD 937 as it appears in *Egil's Saga*; the detailed narrative is frequently used, as it allows the course of the battle to be reconstructed. Certainly, compared to the muddled, poetic description in the Anglo-Saxon Chronicle, it is a model of clarity.

But is it usable? Again, is the course of events described in *Egil's Saga* trustworthy? The simple answer is of course no. Despite the belief that the sagas provide a detailed window on the Viking Age, the truth is they do not. They are, as we shall see, an important historical source, but not for what we want. The problem with the Sagas stems from when they were originally written and why they were originally written.

Written in the late twelfth/early thirteenth century, a number of claims have been made over the years to support their use, none of which are terribly convincing. In terms of the date of writing, it has been argued that this was simply when they were written down and that they are in fact tales that had been told orally for centuries. Unfortunately for this line of argument, it ignores the fact that oral traditions are mutable. Thus, while the germ of the story may remain broadly the same, each new generation tells the story in its own way for its own ends. As a result, details, characters, names, motivations can all change over time to suit the needs, tastes and understanding of the audience. We are thus reading twelfth- or thirteenth-century stories set in the tenth century – not original tenth-century stories. This brings us on to a serious point: the appearance in the sagas of individuals who we know to be genuine historical figures. But what is that to the purpose? Such figures add verisimilitude, nothing more. Modern historical fiction is littered with real people – kings, queens, soldiers, statesmen, etc., the list goes on and on – but we would not pick up a novel written in the twentieth or twenty-first century and use it as evidence for events two, three, or four hundred years ago. Yet this is precisely what we are expected to do with the Sagas. The Sagas are romanticised, fictionalised medieval accounts of the past, written specifically to present an image of a golden past which glorified the ancestors of the writer and the reader at a time when Icelandic society was changing, independence was being lost and direct rule from Norway was being imposed. In this light the Sagas are valuable, but as a source for understanding thirteenth-century Icelandic–Norwegian politics and society and not for casting a light on the earlier Viking age when the stories are set. Saga Iceland was very much a construct of the period when it was written, not when the stories were supposed to have taken place.

Two final, more spurious, arguments in support of the use of Sagas are easily dismissed. The first is circular in that it is contended that the image of Viking society we possess is too close to that presented by the Sagas to be a matter of coincidences – yet this image has been taken in the main from the Sagas and thus we go round and round. Finally, if we do not use the Sagas then we have nothing! Well, nothing written at least. As we shall see, this is also wrong. We have in the West a number of, at times detailed, accounts. They are not necessarily Viking accounts – admittedly, they are usually rather anti-Viking in tone and content – but they are contemporary. As a result they are more considered, reliable and accurate than something written hundreds of years later. There is also the odd bit of contemporary Scandinavian poetry. The Sagas are romantic, fun, enjoyable reads, but this is not *The Man Who Shot Liberty Valance* and we do not need to print the legend.

Before leaving the Sagas and their world behind, we must needs consider the subject of berserkirs. This may seem an odd place to look at such 'creatures', given that they usually feature in their own little section on troop type or organisation, but actually they sit better in a discussion on the authority of the Sagas.

Berserkirs, the bear-skin clad psychopathic warriors of popular imagination, appear in the Sagas not so much as an historical reality but rather as a creature from a mythical past. The best descriptions are in the Sagas of the Ynglings, the Volsungs and of King Hrolf and his champions (*Hrolf's Saga Kraka*), all of which are legendary tales peopled by gods and monsters. Later descriptions paint a far less glamorous image of individuals, men outlawed as a result of violent ferocious attacks. In between the legendary and the sociopathic there is very little. The possibly contemporary poem *Haraldskveaði*, which has been dated to *c.* AD 930, does contain a description of a unit of berserkirs but here they are an ordered company armed with spear and shield, which does not quite fit the popular image.

Representational evidence, particularly the earlier Torslunda die-plates, tend to be circularly interpreted in the light of the Saga evidence, and as a result there is absolutely nothing. Four of the twelve rooks found as a part of the Lewis Chessmen have been identified as berserkirs based solely upon the fact that they are chewing

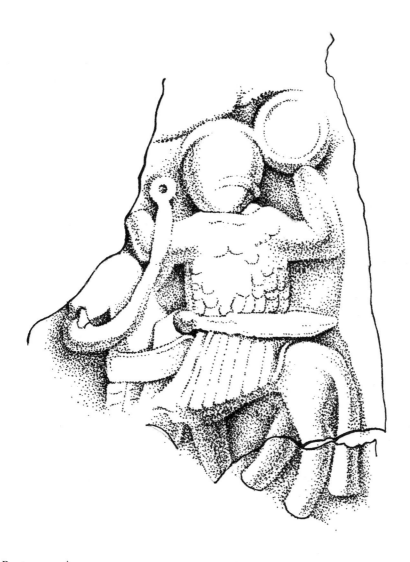

The Repton warrior.

The Viking-period Neston Cross, Fragment 5, Face C. (Redrawn by M. Daniels from White 1986)

the upper rim of their shield, a noted berserkir action. There is nothing wrong with such an identification, however, as the figures are all armoured and helmeted, or coifed in one case, all of which reflected the reality of warfare when the figures were carved, not the image of the berserkir in tales. As for the choice of berserkirs as subjects, this, like the Sagas themselves, probably reflects a popular fictionalised view of the past as well as reflecting the carver's at times comic sense of humour.

More damning for the cult of the berserkir in the Viking Age is the fact that they singularly failed to be mentioned by the clerical chroniclers and annalists of the period. For writers who saw the coming of the Vikings as God's judgment on a sinful world, these inhuman, demonic, bear-clad or naked (berserkirs are sometimes described as such) warriors would, had they existed, surely have made an impression. Certainly, in an earlier age naked Celtic warriors were noted and described by Roman historians of the same period. We are asking too much if we expect such an obvious sign of God's wrath to be overlooked.

The berserkir, like the Sagas to which they belonged, were idealised heroic creations, legendary constructs who had no reality beyond the story or the chessboard. Viking military households were organised along the same lines as their Anglo-Saxon and Frankish counterparts; in this reciprocal culture of gift/counter-gift, noble, heroic individuals such as Bothvar Bjarki, King Hrolf's chief retainer, work as literary constructs. However, the probable reality, the quick-tempered solitary sociopath, had no place in the ordered world of the warband.

Having dismissed what many view as the obvious source of information on the Viking Age, what then do we have? The Viking Age is archaeologically rich and, certainly for Anglo-Saxon England, it reinvigorated the archaeological record. On top of this we have the fact that although the different spheres of Viking activity were to some extent materially distinct, they did not exist in isolation. Thus we see not only an overlap of artefacts but, and this is particularly true in the field of military equipment, a degree of uniformity of style and type with, of course, regional variations. Such variations, for example the use of scale armour and maces in the East, did have the possibility, albeit on a small scale, of being transferred to the West. Equally, the Vikings were no more immune than the rest of the West in the face of the rise of pan-European fashions, which in military equipment terms equates to the conical helmet and the kite shield. On a slightly larger scale, ship finds from Gokstad, Oseberg and Roskilde, to name but the three most famous, have, along with a number of other ship finds, helped us to paint a picture of maritime warfare, which would be impossible without these finds.

We are also fairly well served by the representational evidence. For besides classic images such as the Lindisfarne Stone, with its very warlike band of Vikings, images from Brompton, Sockburn and Middleton, along with for example the Gosforth and Neston crosses, give an insight not only into styles of dress and equipment but also into the uses of such equipment, as well as offering an insight into the more controversial area of mounted combat.

Alongside the sculptural evidence, manuscript illustrations paint a picture of the warfare of the day, while the end of the period is perhaps best, and most famously, represented by the Bayeux Tapestry. The tapestry, although usually seen as a source simply for the end of Anglo-Saxon England, does also in fact depict two armies, both of whom have to some degree Viking ancestors. The English, or more correctly the Anglo-Danish, force led by Harold II Godwinson was the product of not only the English tradition of warfare but also of the results of the two Viking ages and the Danish conquest of AD 1013–16. Meanwhile, its opponents, the Norman army of William the Bastard, were in many ways of more direct Viking descent, albeit with a more wholesale adoption of the latest trends in European military tactical thinking. All parties on the tapestry betray the influence of the latest fashions in eleventh-century military equipment.

The archaeological evidence is in many ways the Vikings speaking directly to us in terms of their tastes, styles and habits and the same is also true to some extent of the representational evidence, although in the latter case more so in respect of Viking Age sculptures than with the manuscript illustrations as the Vikings were at times more probably the patrons and producers of such carvings.

The inadmissibility of the Sagas as evidence is not as grievous as many people would think. For as has already been argued, the loss of evidence of no worth is no loss. Nor does this mean that there is no literary evidence for this period; on the contrary – there is a lot of contemporary written evidence.

Certainly in England the late Anglo-Saxon period is better served by its written as opposed to its archaeological evidence. However, in this we see the rub for England and, indeed, Western Europe is well served by a number of, at times detailed, accounts of Viking activity, albeit not written from the point of view of, or by, the Vikings. The clerical writers of the various annals and chronicles were biased, indeed obviously so, against the Vikings, whom they saw as agents of a wrathful God. However, this does not stop them being an invaluable source of evidence for the Viking period. This is particularly true of England, which is one of the main reasons why this work in the main concentrates on it. For besides the various of manuscripts of the Anglo-Saxon Chronicle, we have also the *Life of King Alfred*, the *Life of Edward the Confessor*, and the *Encomium Emmae Reginae*, as well as the poems of the battles of Maldon and Brunanburgh, to name but the more obvious and famous works.

Supporting these, and again why we have in the main concentrated primarily on the Vikings of Western Europe, we have Frankish works such as the Annals of Fulda, Abbo of Saint-Germain-Des-Prés, *Bella Parisiacae Urbis* and of course the letters of Alcuin, alongside various Irish annals such as those of Clonmacnoise.

Nor were the Vikings themselves wholly silent. However, the fragments of Scandinavian verse quoted are used cautiously, as the dating and reliability of such works is open to question. Despite all of this, the weight of evidence is not at times overwhelming. As with all historical-archaeological periods, there are still gaps. However, we are in a position to paint a convincing picture of Viking warfare in England.

3

The Wrath of God

Then from the rocky shore the ward of Scyldings,
Whose duty was the sea-cliffs guard, saw borne over bulwark bright shields, excellent
war-gear.
Curiosity pressed his thoughts, who were these men.

Beowulf, lines 229–233

Ironically, the Viking Age opened like a bizarre, bloody parody of *Beowulf*. The causes of the Viking Age have been viewed as many and varied. Thus we see the events that are to follow arguably resulting from political changes in Scandinavia caused by the coalescing of smaller polities and the creation of kingdoms and by the inability of existing states to combat piracy, as did Rome at the high point of its empire. The waning of the empire and the failure of successor states to emulate its power and control created a vacuum, which in this case the Vikings exploited. Economic reasons have also been advanced: by the late eighth century the successors to Rome, if not as powerful, were resurgent in economic terms and rich, poorly defended targets are always a temptation. Or we could turn to an Elizabethan parallel and see it as a result of weak central control of the fringes in the various Scandinavian monarchies, which allowed those who went 'a-Viking' to indulge in a mixture of trading, colonisation and piratical enterprises, depending upon the situation. The argument that this was a pagan backlash against the muscular Christianity of Charlemagne has also been advanced. Here, however, we are not in the main interested in cause; our concern is effect.

The first attack in AD 789 saw the death of a reeve, a royal official; the second attack, a few years later in AD 793, sent shock waves across the Christian world. The sack of the monastery at Lindisfarne, or Holy Island, is usually taken, albeit incorrectly, as the opening of the Viking Age. Why the event, was viewed at the time as so horrendous is difficult to fully understand at this remove of time.

The target itself, the monastery, was in many ways what we today would call a 'soft target'. Yet that in itself is not enough. The nature of the target also does not single it out as special. That good Christian King Ecgfrith was perfectly content to allow the sack of his co-religionists' churches; admittedly they were Irish and thus foreign, but the attacks were in all respects really no different to the sack of Lindisfarne. Possibly, the cause of consternation for many stemmed from the fact that the attackers in AD 793 were *heathen*.

Yet were they possibly doing God's work?

> For the Wrath of God is revealed from Heaven against all ungodliness and unrighteousness of man, who hold the truth in unrighteousness.
>
> Romans 1:18

This is how Alcuin at the court of Charlemagne viewed the beginning of what would turn out to be the first of many attacks. In this he was no different to Augustine of Hippo, who in earlier centuries had seen the turmoil affecting the Roman world as God's judgement upon the sinfulness of mankind.

Of course, today in military terms we see the opening acts of the Viking Age not as an act of God, but rather as a result of the problems encountered by a rich, ordered polity in the face of raiders. Indeed, for the Anglo-Saxons the wheel had come full circle. The English kingdoms sprang from the similar raids in the fifth century upon the Roman provinces of Britain. Now, in the eighth and ninth centuries, the descendants of these raiders were faced with the same problem as their Roman predecessors, and like the Romans, their success were limited.

After 789 and 793 we see, according to the E manuscript of the Anglo-Saxon Chronicle, a raid ending in disaster for the Vikings. In AD 794 [796] St Paul's at Jarrow, the Venerable Bede's old monastery, was sacked.

> And there one of their commanders was killed, and also some of their ships were broken up by bad weather, and many of them drowned there; and some came to the shore alive and then were immediately killed at the river mouth.

Whether the Viking commander was killed in the raid or in the storm is both unknown and unknowable – either is possible. Even without the storm, the mouth of the River Tyne is treacherous. The Jarrow raid was for the English at least followed by a hiatus. The early 800s saw, according to our sources, Viking raids on Scotland and Ireland. The English were left at peace and had to content themselves with killing themselves and their British neighbours. In AD 832 [835], according to the Anglo-Saxon Chronicle A manuscript, the 'heathen' Vikings returned, ravaging the Isle of Sheppey. This gap of nearly forty years is not readily explainable. The obvious conclusion to jump to is that our sources are deficient and this may, of course, to some extent be true. Low-level raids may have occurred and simply not been recorded, or the records simply do not survive. Equally, given that we know that attacks occurred in other parts of the British Isles, specifically Ireland but also Scotland, Orkney, Shetland and the Western Isles, it may be that easier targets were sought and found by the Vikings. Although storms and geography far more than military prowess on the part of the English explain the failure of the Jarrow raid, this desire for easier, safer targets, may have been compounded by the presence and power of Charlemagne's Francia just across the Channel. By the 830s AD, however, Charlemagne was dead and the power of his empire, wracked as it was by dynastic squabbling, was on the wane. As a result Francia found itself a target; but the rich pickings of South and Eastern England now also found themselves vulnerable and exposed to renewed Viking attention. England and its various kingdoms did not exist in isolation, and as we shall see again, most notably in AD 1066, events on the continent could have a marked effect on the course of English history.

As the various manuscripts of the Anglo-Saxon Chronicle make clear, the 830s and 840s were dominated by the depredations of the Vikings. Yet the Chronicle annals for the years AD 833 to AD 845 do not paint a picture of overwhelming Viking supremacy. Indeed, if anything, the laurels are equally shared. Thus we see the Viking victorious in AD 833 [836] and AD 840 [843] at Carhampton and at Portland in AD 840 [837], as well as the 'Great Slaughters' which took place in London, Quentovic and Rochester. However, alongside these we see English victories at Hingston Down in AD 835 [838], when King Egbert of Wessex defeated a combined force of Welsh and Vikings; at Southampton in AD 837 [840]; and at the mouth of the River Parret in AD 845.

Why one side had the victory in these engagements is not now a question we can answer. Guesses can of course be hazarded, but that is all they would be – guesses; we lack the evidence to go beyond saying simply who won and who lost. What we can say is that in AD 851 the strategic situation changed. The year was on the face of it one of mixed fortunes, with English success at Wicca's stronghold (wheresoever that might be), at Sandwich, and at another unidentified site, Oak Field, being counter-balanced by the storming of Canterbury and London, as well as by the defeat of King Beorhtwulf. What, however, marks this year out from the preceding decade or so of increasing Viking activity was the fact that for the first time a Viking force overwintered in England. This first overwintering was at Thanet; the second, in AD 853, was at Shepey. Both locations are, of course, easily defended, but this is beside the point. What these events do show is that any simple win/lose listing does not, indeed cannot, convey the whole picture. Certainly neither side had proved itself invincible, and that state of events would remain the same throughout the whole of the Viking period. However, what we do see in AD 851 [850] is the initiative passing to the Vikings. Why this occurs is harder to say and we can only surmise. Possibly the Vikings were able to deploy larger forces; certainly the sack of London, Canterbury and, in AD 860, Winchester show that their targets were becoming larger. Equally certain is the fact that larger raids coupled with battlefield success, even against royal armies, would have had a detrimental effect on English morale. For even though England did not at this point exist as a unified kingdom, news of these events would have spread.

This lack of unity, coupled with the fact that purely internal politics did not abate, would prove fatal for the kingdoms of the English. The first of the dominos to fall was Northumbria. The Great Raiding Army of AD 866 [865] can be seen as a direct result of Frankish success and English failure. Strengthened defences provided an effective response to the Viking menace. Thus England and the English, in the face of strengthened and effective Frankish resistance, proved an easier and more tempting target. Despite the fact that Northumbria at this time was wracked by civil war, East Anglia appears to have been militarily the weaker kingdom and the Vikings exploited this to their advantage. Overwintering in East Anglia, the once-mighty kingdom chose to appease the invaders. The horses which the Viking leadership demanded as the price for peace gave the invaders the strategic mobility they required and, as we shall see, this would come back to haunt East Anglia. The following year, AD 867 [866], the Great Raiding Army took the city of York. Laying aside their differences, Osberht and Ælla, rival kings of Northumbria, united and sought to retake the city. Disaster ensued; both kings and a great number of Northumbrians, so the chronicles tell us, were slaughtered. York was now effectively a Viking city.

Invasion facilitated settlement; however, here we are not seeing the all-encompassing control we associate with the domination of Wessex, something, ironically, the Vikings Wars made possible. Nor are we seeing the sort of conquest we associate with the Anglo-Danish Wars and the rule of Swein and Cnut. In these cases we see the total replacement of one ruler by another; in the late AD 860s we are looking at hegemonic control, with an eye very much to the richer south of the country.

With York secure and a puppet ruler installed, the Great Raiding Army took up winter quarters in Nottingham in the heart of Mercia. While it has been argued that at this stage Mercia was still militarily formidable, the fact remains that a joint Mercian and West Saxon force was unable to dislodge the Vikings. Nor were they able to prevent the Vikings crossing Mercian territory as they willed. Mercia's inability to curtail the invaders proved fatal for East Anglia. In AD 870, leaving York, they overwintered in Thetford. Probably realising that this time the Vikings were intent on conquest Edmund, King of East Anglia, attacked. The subsequent English defeat saw not only the death of the King but also the end of the kingdom as a political entity. For unlike Northumbria, or for that matter Viking-controlled Mercia, no puppet was installed. Instead, as the Anglo-Saxon Chronicle makes clear, the Vikings 'conquered all that land'. Mercia's turn came in AD 874; Burhred the king was driven out, subsequently settling in Rome, and Ceolwulf, remembered by history as 'a foolish king's thegn' was installed as ruler.

Prior to the fall of Mercia we see a number of attacks on Wessex, with AD 871 [870], the year of Alfred's accession, being especially prominent in our sources. The defence of Wessex, particularly under Alfred, is legend and while it is undeniable that it put up the staunchest defence, it is equally true that the tide of circumstance was turning in their favour. Thus, even though the West Saxon victory at Ashdown in AD 871 showed that the Vikings were not invincible, the same year saw King

Æthelred and his brother Alfred defeated at Reading and Merton, while Alfred, after he had succeeded his brother as king, faced defeat at Viking hands at Wilton. After the fall of Mercia, Wessex stands out as the obvious target; instead, however, the raiders turned north and east. Having taken winter quarters at Repton in AD 875 [874], part of the army under Guthrum, Oscytel and Anund went to Cambridge, while Halfdan took a force into the as yet un-subdued north of Northumbria. The initial conquest of this kingdom had concentrated on the southern or Deiran half of the kingdom and now it was Bernicia's turn. The image of Wessex and its plucky king standing isolated and alone, the last of the English kingdoms, very much fits with our vision of our history. Further reinforcing this point of view is the idea of Alfred as the 'founder' of the Royal Navy, the senior service, which over the centuries had poured scorn on foreign tyrants' vaunting ambitions. Sadly, the reality is slightly more prosaic. English kings nominally ruled in Mercia, Northumbria and even, it has been argued, in East Anglia, although the real power in these areas lay in Viking hands. Equally, these earlier successes, coupled with the concomitant settlement, had spread Viking power and numbers out, although these were still formidable.

Guthrum's first attempt on Wessex was not a resounding success. Instead, we see stalemate. Wareham and Exeter were both taken by the Vikings. On each occasion the invaders were bottled up by the West Saxons, and in each case both sides agreed terms. Neither possessed the strength to overcome the other. Spread across large parts of eastern, central and southern England, the 'all-conquering' Great Raiding Army was neither as large, nor as splendid, as when it first landed in East Anglia.

Attempting to break the stalemate, Guthrum attacked in the middle of winter. Surprising Alfred at Chippenham sometime after Twelfth Night, January AD 878, Guthrum succeeded in taking most of Wessex but failed to take the king. This was the nadir of Wessex's fortunes. Alfred was a fugitive, the leading men of the kingdom had either fled abroad or submitted to the Vikings and a second Viking force which had overwintered in Dyfed effected a landing in Devon in order to carve up the rest of the kingdom. The Great Raiding Army's conquest of the kingdoms of the English seemed complete. But it was not quite complete enough. It is true that the failure to capture Alfred need not necessarily have been disastrous to the Viking cause. Burhred of Mercia in similar circumstances had fled to Rome and Alfred himself may have been given similar council; he may even have contemplated such a fate with no need for external voices to suggest it.

Guthrum, however, did not understand his opponent. Equally, Alfred was no Burhred and that indeed is a part of his legend. Attempts have been made to increase the prominence of Edward, Alfred's son and heir, to move him out of the shadow of the father and to correctly attribute deeds, specifically building projects, to Edward that had formally been assumed to be Alfredian. Such actions are of course right and proper, for in his own right Edward was a great king by the measures of the age; he, to quote the *Beowulf* poet, 'dragged away the mead benches from bands of foes, from many tribes'. However, the firm foundations upon which Edward built were Alfred's.

The Vikings' hold on Wessex in AD 878 rapidly began to unravel. The Western force was defeated by the men of Devon at Contisbury, while Alfred, firmly ensconced within the marshes of Athelney, proceeded to fortify his new dwelling and launch a series of raids against his enemies. Still, for the Vikings under Guthrum the situation was not entirely irretrievable. This was very much an age of battles. All Guthrum needed to do was bring Alfred to 'the place of slaughter' and defeat him. The long-expected engagement took place at Edington in Wiltshire, where after fierce fighting God granted the victory to the men of Wessex, or so Asser articulated it. The Vikings then suffered a dreadful pursuit to their stronghold, which was possibly Chippenham; all who were caught were killed. There, after fourteen days' hard siege in which starvation proved to be the Anglo-Saxons' best weapon, Guthrum and the remains of his army sought peace. Guthrum and the thirty leading men of the army also agreed to receive baptism. The Viking conquest of England was over and Wessex was saved – for now.

As it turns out, AD 878 was the high tide of Viking conquest in England during the first Viking Age. Wessex was safe and the way was paved, ironically, thanks to the Vikings, for it to go on to greater things. Despite the obvious success of AD 871 and the strategic surprise of AD 878, the Viking assault upon Wessex failed for three reasons. Firstly, neither side was tactically superior to the other and as a result at Edington the victory lay with the side with the higher morale. This was undoubtedly the West Saxons, who had more to lose in defeat and, as a consequence, went on to win the engagement. The second factor was numerical; the earlier stalemates at Wareham and Exeter suggest parity of forces. As we have already seen, the Great Raiding Army, although by no means an insignificant force, was as a result of its own success not as great as it once was. It is, though, potentially arguable that the great force which first landed in East Anglia in AD 866 [865] would have been more than a match for whatever force Alfred chose to field. However, after over a decade of conquest, warfare, settlement and division, its numbers, even accounting for new groups joining, were not what they once were. Finally, we have the person of the king himself. Alfred was an interfering busybody whose subjects would probably have had a far less costly (in the purse) time under Viking rule. However, he was a tenacious leader of men, a warrior, a victorious war leader, in short a great king, as Guthrum found to his cost. A lesser man, and here we think of Æthelred II, would have fled abroad. Guthrum's underestimation of his opponent, coupled with the other factors, proved fatal to the Viking cause.

Viking attacks on Wessex were for the time being in abeyance. However, that is not to say that all Viking activity ceased, as indeed Asser makes clear; for the time being such activity was confined, as far as we are concerned, to settlement in East Anglia and attacks on Francia. The latter was obviously a much more alluring target, particularly now that England was either under Viking control or, in the case of Wessex, too strong to assail.

The situation changed in AD 885 when a raiding army which had spent a year at Amiens split into two. One force went on to besiege Louvain, the other Rochester. The ensuing hostilities mostly consisted of English victories. Rochester was relieved and the attackers, abandoning their horses and fortifications, fled. Some, however, remained and with the aid of Vikings from East Anglia raided south of the Thames. This gave Alfred the excuse to attack East Anglian territory. Alfred's fleet was victorious; unfortunately for them, on the way home they fell in with what the Anglo-Saxon Chronicle (A & E manuscripts, 885 [884]) calls a 'great raiding ship-army of Vikings, and then fought against them the same day, and the Danish had the victory.'

However, Alfred's taking of London in AD 886 [885] set the seal on what could be seen as the West Saxon King's overall victory and appears to have allowed him to very much dictate terms once again to Guthrum, who was now King of East Anglia. The death of Guthrum in AD 890 did not change the status quo. What did was the arrival from the continent in AD 893 [892] of a new Great Raiding Army.

The actions of the new Great Raiding Army are in some ways like those of Æthelred II approximately a hundred years later, in that we see a great deal of power and potential poorly directed and coming to nought. For despite allying themselves to the Vikings of York and East Anglia, they never succeeded in their objectives, being constantly frustrated by Alfred's forces or, when they moved north to Chester, by the forces of Ealdorman Æthelred of Mercia, Alfred's son-in-law. This is not to say that the Great Raiding Army and its allies did not do a lot of damage. However, the new system of fortifications and the reforms to the West Saxon military structure instituted by Alfred both contained the threat and allowed forces to be kept in the field for longer and more effectively than previously.

Thus they had failed to take Wessex, had marched north to Chester, faced starvation and an abortive raid on Gwynedd, returned to the south-east, lost most of their ships to the garrison of London and finally succeeded in establishing winter quarters on the Severn at Bridgnorth. By AD 896, foiled yet again by Alfred's army, they dispersed. Some went north to York, others east to East Anglia, while the remainder took ship to Francia. At the beginning of the First Viking age, even at the arrival of the first Great Raiding Army, the initiative had lain with the Vikings. They were able to deploy overwhelming force against an enemy quite unprepared to deal with a threat on this scale. Numbers do not guarantee victory – but they help. But by this point it was over a century since the first Viking attacks and over three decades since the arrival of the first Great Raiding Army. Thus the successes of the 860s and 870s, built upon shock, terror and the exploitation of existing weaknesses, were not about to be replicated in the 890s. Wessex was now too strong and too well defended, while that part of Mercia under the control of Ealdorman Æthelred was supported by the might of Wessex. The failure of the new Great Raiding Army moved the initiative firmly over to the English.

Alfred died in AD 899 and was succeeded by his son Edward, who assumed the title 'King of the Anglo-Saxons'.

The next half of the century saw the re-conquest, the unification of England under the rule of the royal house of Wessex. Such a process would in all probability have taken place, at some point, without the Viking period ever having happened. However, without the impact of the Vikings it is more debatable as to which of the Anglo-Saxon Kingdoms would have taken the lead. The Vikings did impact upon, and in many ways facilitated, the rise of Wessex and the formation of England by effectively removing all of the kingdom of Wessex's long-standing rivals.

In many ways the speed of the English reconquest is remarkable. Yet, as with the earlier Viking conquest, the Danelaw was no more a single united entity than Anglo-Saxon England was on the eve of the Viking age.

Thus, by AD 920 Edward had conquered all of the land south of the Humber. English Mercia had been annexed on the death of Æthelred in AD 911. Whereas his father had mainly, and understandably, concentrated on defending and strengthening Wessex, Edward used his patrimony as a secure base from which to project the growing power of Wessex. Thus, we see from our sources that Edward was not content to simply raid, but to raid extensively. Excused as a result of provocation, such raids helped weaken Viking-controlled areas and allow for the borders of Wessex to be pushed further and further. The vision of a single England was to some extent articulated by Bede, adopted by Alfred and made real by Alfred's descendants. Consolidation came via the medium of fortress building. As a result, like his father before him, he handed over a (mostly) secure legacy. Edward's annexation of Mercia was not universally popular within the former kingdom, although problems were to all intents and purposes erased by the accession in AD 924 of Edward's son Athelstan, who had been raised in Mercia by his aunt, Æthelflæd, Lady of the Mercians.

By AD 927 the task appeared complete. Athelstan drove out King Guthfrith and succeeded to the Kingdom of Northumbria. Certainly all seemed well at first. In AD 934 Athelstan, Viking-like, raided Scotland with both an army and fleet. Attempts were of course made to reverse the trend. The most famous of these was at Brunabrugh, location unknown, in AD 937. Here, a coalition of Vikings from Dublin and northern England, allied with King Constantine of Scotland and his men, was crushed by Athelstan. The victory was lauded as a great triumph, which indeed it was. It was not, as it turned out, strategically decisive, but then few great victories ever are. Two years later Athelstan was dead and York, the prize of the Brunabrugh campaign, was back under Viking control.

Olaf Guthfrithsson's success proved transitory; his death in AD 941 ushered in a succession of lesser rulers. Thus by the end of King Edmund's reign, the north-east Midlands, which had rebelled, were back under control and as a result of the removal of Olaf Guthfrithsson from the stage, Wessex exerted hegemonic, if not actual physical, control of the north.

The Anglo-Saxon Chronicle is remarkably prosaic about the end of the first Viking age.

954. Here the Northumbrians drove out Eric, and Eadred succeeded to the Kingdom of Northumbria.

Tradition nicely rounds off this story with the death of Eric in the Battle of Stainmore in Westmorland. We lack contemporary accounts of the event, or for that matter the fate of Eric; this is not to say that the battle did not happen, although we should not accept it as an indisputable fact. To all intents and purposes the first Viking age was over: it ended, surprisingly given the state of affairs at times, with the English, in the form of the King of Wessex, victorious. Viking activity did not of course cease, but for the time being England was at peace.

To us the second Viking age, like the first, is explicable in socio-political terms. To the Anglo-Saxons it was explicable, again like the first, in terms of sin. Wulfstan, who was among other things Archbishop of York, explained in his now famous *Sermon of 'Wolf' to the English when the Danes persecuted them most, which was in the year 1014 from the incarnation of our Lord Jesus Christ* that the return of the Vikings was God's judgement and vengeance upon the English for their many sins, particularly and generally against ecclesiastical property, and specifically for that most terrible of crimes, regicide – the murder of God's anointed. King Edward, subsequently known as 'the Martyr', and the son of Edgar, was murdered on the evening of 18 March 978 at Corfe in Dorset.

Militarily, at one level the pressures faced by the Anglo-Saxon state at the beginning of the second Viking age were minor and local, and the response of necessity needed to be proportionate to the perceived threat. Equally, the state as a whole was in an invidious position. For just like their predecessors, the Imperial Roman Army, the armed forces of Anglo-Saxon England were required to defend and protect a rich, ordered polity against an increasingly successful and determined force of sea-borne raiders. Unfortunately, unlike their Roman counterparts they did not control both sides of the Channel, although they did try diplomatically to resolve this problem.

Turning to the various manuscripts of the Anglo-Saxon Chronicle, we see the worst deed done since the coming of the English to Britain, namely the murder of King Edward in 978. The 979 entry in the C manuscript is dominated by a portentous 'bloody cloud', and from 980 onwards, but a little way into the reign of the new king, Æthelred, we have a litany of raids. In 988 and 991 we have two English defeats and their accompanying slaughters, the first at Watchet and the second, more famous, one at Maldon. The list continues and the pattern remains the same. Raid and ravaging, punctuated by English defeats.

Examining the defeats is hard in specific terms. The Anglo-Saxon Chronicle A manuscript entry for 1001 tells us that at Ætheling's Valley in Hampshire a battle was fought; it lists the prominent English dead and then goes on to say that 'there were many more of the Danish killed, though they had possession of the place of slaughter'. The Danes equally 'had possession of the place of slaughter' later that same year at Pinhoe. In terms of the tactical formations used, the numbers involved, the presence or absence of surprise, we lack all such information. What we can surmise is that the English failure may well have been grounded in low morale and poor leadership, which were themselves the result of two decades of defeat and failure. High enemy and low English morale may, like the view of the Norman invincibility that prevailed after Hastings, have resulted from the apparent inability of the *fyrd* to either prevent raids, or if intercepted, to defeat the raiders.

Leadership at a local level at times appears decisive and resolute, if not always successful, with the example of Byrthtnoth, as well as of Ulfcytel of East Anglia and Uhtred of Northumbria, standing out, although in these cases we are again reduced to lists of engagements and, if lucky, sparse details of actions. In 1006, for example, Simeon of Durham relates that Uhtred of Bamburgh raised the siege of Durham and placed the heads of the vanquished Scots on the city's ramparts in grim warning.

At a national level, however, things were different. In recent years, attempts have been made to rehabilitate Æthelred II, the 'Unready'; the argument goes that he was an effective governor, legislator and administrator. But at the end of the day this counts for nothing. A king was expected to drag 'away the mead benches from bands of foes' (*Beowulf*, lines 4–5); instead, foes dragged away Æthelred's mead bench.

> In that year [991] it was first decided tax be paid to the Danish men because of the great terror which they wrought along the sea coast. That was at first ten thousand pounds.
>
> Anglo-Saxon Chronicle, E manuscript

The payment of *Danegeld* remains to this day a controversial topic. At one level it was successful; at another, it did no more than increase and excite the cupidity of the raiders. The payment of subsidies to potentially hostile elements beyond the frontiers of civilisation to buy peace, to support and enhance friendly elements or to hire mercenaries (auxiliaries) was nothing new – the Romans were famous for it. The Romans, however, employed it with a carrot (cash) and stick (Imperial Roman Army) mentality. Sadly, the Æthelredian version, by contrast, was more reward than punishment. The stick in Æthelred's case was at times the military force and loyalty of those Vikings who had been paid with the carrot. In some ways, the policy worked: Olaf of Norway was permanently bought off, and Thorkell the Tall proved loyal; Pallig, however, did not. In other ways, the policy failed to protect the country. It did not stop the raids, and subsequent payments were larger. The buying of peace at national and local level (East Anglia attempted it in 1004) would have been more widely known and, militarily, would have impacted badly on the morale of any English force.

In 1000 Æthelred campaigned in the north. The various chronicle sources tinge his endeavours with failure. As to the campaign's purpose, was the ravaging of Cumbria, Strathclyde and the Isle of Man intended as a show of strength generally, or just in the north? It is impossible to say for certain, although the latter case is more likely than the former. English military efforts reached a new nadir in 1006. Æthelred, it would appear, was collecting food rents in Shropshire while a Viking raiding force based on the Isle of Wight ravaged, controlled and drew supplies and render from Wessex. As Tolkien, albeit in a work of fiction, *The Silmarillion*, noted: 'A king is he that he can hold his own, or else his title is in vain.' Wessex was very much his own. The events of 1006 showed that Æthelred's title was vain. Equally, the tenth-century achievements of the House of Cedric were unraveling. England was beginning to look ripe for the picking.

Other initiatives both diplomatic and administrative impacted militarily on Æthelred's kingdom. His marriage in 1002 to Emma of Normandy made a degree of sense in that it closed the Duchy as a safe haven for Viking raiders; it also, as it turned out, provided him with a safe haven in 1013. Equally, the 1002 St Brice's Day (13 November) Massacre can at best be described as an unsound policy. This attempt to massacre all the Danes living in the kingdom (ethnic cleansing, as it would be labelled in modern parlance) was, like the 1572 St Bartholomew's Day Massacre, most probably successful in those urban areas where the ethnic mix was more English than Danish. In the Danelaw, the Anglo-Danish north, it is more unlikely that the order was executed, and it is more likely that it resulted in the breeding of an ill name and an evil reputation for Æthelred, which would have disastrous results in 1013. It is equally questionable how easy it was to carry out such a policy, even in the south of the country. However, it does not appear to have been attempted in Oxford at least. Alongside the story of the Danes burnt to death in St Frideswide's in Oxford, a number of bodies have recently been excavated from the Kendrew Quadrangle site in the centre of the city. The bodies of at least twenty individuals were found in a mass grave. A number show evidence of traumatic, possibly weapons related deaths, and all have been tentatively dated to c. AD 1000, thus nicely fitting with the events of AD 1002, although whether they were killed as part of the events of St Brice's Day in that year or whether they belong to the Danish reprisals of AD 1009 or some other unrecorded event is both unknown and unknowable.

Æthelred's great fleet of 1009 was a testimony to the strength and power of the English state. The fact that internal squabbles among the ruling elite caused the fleet to fragment, to be partially destroyed by a storm and, most damningly, for only part of it to see action and for that action to be against the south coast of England itself, points to weakness at the very top. Equally, the construction of new *burhs* and the refurbishment of existing ones shows that attempts were made to increase the kingdom's defensive capabilities. However, like the great self-destructing fleet of 1009, such efforts came to naught.

A lack of leadership and internal divisions among the ruling elite, which led to a lack of trust and a failure to co-operate, combined to produce a lack of coherent defence policy, with the events of 1013 as the outcome. The lack of a coherent strategy comes across in the fact that the 1008 legislation, the 1009 fleet, and the building and refurbishment of *burhs* all appear as one-offs, seemingly unconnected to the successful application of force. Meanwhile resistance, such as that in East Anglia in 1004, against Swein of Denmark was co-ordinated at a local level. It is true that at first the raiding problem was a local problem and needed to be dealt with at a local level; by 1004, however, the problem was national and needed to be dealt with using national resources. However, at this higher level, resistance was non-existent and all too often raiding-armies (as the Anglo-Saxon Chronicle calls them) appear to have overwintered in England unimpeded by the royal host.

England was finally picked in 1013. Swein of Denmark mounted a successful campaign of conquest which owed as much to the size and quality of his army as to English failures both political (the internal squabbles, intrigues, coups and murders) and military (the inability to either stop, defeat or deter the raiders). The political failures of the English state stemmed in part from Edgar's early death, while military failures had been the pattern since 980; however, both were so much a part of Æthelred's kingship that he cannot and indeed should not escape blame – he as king was ultimately responsible for the safe guard of his realm. Swein's initial attempt to land at Sandwich failed; he rapidly moved his fleet to the Humber and the more friendly Anglo-Danish north, which quickly submitted and took him as king. As a result of this shrewd move his next advance south, this time overland, succeeded and the south of the kingdom followed the north's lead. London resisted, but Æthelred's failure to take the field and his subsequent flight to Normandy made further resistance futile.

The language of the Anglo-Saxon Chronicle manuscripts remains at times the same, even though the circumstances are different. Thus we see, unsurprisingly, stock phrases used. In this case Swein's army is described as a 'raiding-army' and while this is true to some extent (all armies in this period were raiding armies), the fact remains that we have moved away from the diverse forces which made up the 'Great Raiding-Army' of earlier centuries. Yes, the composition of contingents would be very similar; however, the force Swein used was the royal army of the kingdom with a single will, Swein's, directing it to a single purpose – the conquest of England.

Swein's, Cnut's, and Harald Hardrada's forces are all described as Viking forces. Harald Hardrada is even described as one of the greatest Vikings of the whole age, while Cnut is seen as the most successful. But by this stage we are not seeing raiding for its own ends, or even attempts to take part of the land to rule and settle; rather these are now wars between kingdoms with survival being the goal of the English and empire-building being the result sought by the successive Danish and Norwegian monarchs.

Swein's sudden death on 3 February 1014 led to what can only be described as an unexpected military highpoint in Æthelred's career. Invited back, but on conditions, Æthelred and his host caught Cnut, Swein's son and successor in England, unawares and unable to gather his strength. Cnut and his Danish forces fled, leaving their English supporters to be 'raided and burned and killed' (Anglo-Saxon Chronicle E ms, 1014) by Æthelred's men. Such punishment of his own people may seem harsh; it was, however, the price that was paid at the time for being unsuccessful in treason. For Æthelred, the success and the reprieve were temporary.

Monarchy, and particularly medieval monarchy, was martial. The defence of the realm took precedence and the king, even as late as the Hanoverian period, took the field against a foreign enemy. Richard III, may have been the last King of England to lead his knights in a charge into the heart of the enemy's ranks, at Bosworth in 1485, but it was George II some 258 years later at Dettingen, in 1743, who last commanded a British army in battle. Æthelred II, it would appear, did not understand or could not come to grips with this most important aspect of kingship. Beowulf, although he was an old man, went alone into the dragon's lair because he saw it as his duty as king to protect his people from all threats. While this may today be seen as an extreme example, it must be remembered that the poem, which started with Scyld Scefing and ends with Beowulf's last fight, death and funeral, provided a behavioural model to aspire to. Æthelred, by his failure to join his army in 1016 (and the army expected his presence and ceased to exist without him), and by his failure to take the field against Cnut, fell far short of expectations and it is an indelible stain on his character. Excuses of old age and ill health will not wash; kings, even though blind, have still fought in battles. The requirements of heroic leadership and the warrior ethic in a martial aristocracy and society were undoubtedly hard and unremitting in their intolerance of failure and kings such as Æthelred II and Edward II who have failed to live up to such standards have been harshly judged, and rightly so. Such men were expected to lead and to die at the front; failure to do so, or an apparent reluctance to do so on Æthelred's part, damned both his kingdom and his reputation.

The reign of Edmund 'Ironside', though short, was active and as a result it stands in marked contrast to that of his father. Certainly he was still plagued with internal political problems; militarily, however, he took to the field. Again, we return to the old problem of sketchy or non-existent details and simple lists of engagements. In organisational and administrative terms, the ability of Edmund to raise armies and the ease with which he did so points to the impressive institutional structures of the late Anglo-Saxon state. Edmund also seems, from the D manuscript of the Anglo-Saxon Chronicle, to have used his forces well and successfully. However, other than the fact that he engaged in a mounted pursuit when driving the Danes to Sheppey, tactical details are lost to us. The Danes, during their siege of London in the same year, appear to have employed circumvallation and used warships as platforms from which assaults on riverside fortifications could be launched. We have no record of the English employing the same techniques, although there is no reason why they could not in similar circumstances have followed, or copied, the Danes' example. Edmund's last great battle, Ashingdon, was lost through treachery, and that is all that can be said of it. As for the stability of his subsequent treaty with Cnut, while it is unlikely to have lasted, it was in the event never put to the test. Edmund died on 30 November 1016 and Cnut succeeded to the whole kingdom.

The mismanagement and unrealised potential, respectively, of the previous two reigns did not occur under Cnut. However, it is likely that had he lived longer himself, his great creation would have partially unravelled before his eyes. As it was, Cnut, who became more English than the English, stands as one of the most successful medieval monarchs and certainly as the most successful Viking ever, for he created what was in effect an empire. Ruling all of England from late 1016, he inherited Denmark in 1019, conquered Norway in 1028 and even ruled parts of Sweden.

However, from the accession of Cnut in AD 1016 until the Battle of Hastings in AD 1066 we are now looking in England at the history of the Anglo-Danish state, and then on into the history of Anglo-Norman England. Cnut's success marks the close to all intents and purposes of the second Viking age. Subsequent attacks or potential attacks on England, such as Harthacnut's planned invasion of 1039/40 and the almost-civil-war of 1052 were concerned with power, status and the rightful succession. The latter was of course also the cause of the events of 1066. Thus, even if we view the tactics as the same as the earlier Viking ages, the nature of the protagonists, as in 1013–16, had changed.

4

Bright Wargear

There many men lay slain by spears, and northern warriors shot down despite their shields, and Scotsmen too.

Battle of Brunanburh, lines 17–19

Military equipment, the bright wargear of the chapter title, was in many ways remarkably constant in form and function over the period. As well as performing a military purpose it fulfilled a second important role as a status symbol, with the richer and more exotic the style the greater the apparent wealth and prestige of the owner. However, in the gift–counter-gift culture which existed, the corollary just made was not necessarily always true, as service or deed rendered could be well rewarded. However, the record of such deeds is now lost and we are as a result left with the more simplistic interpretation that the wealth of weapons and armour equated to the status of the owner.

When we turn to form, we are in many cases merely cataloguing the vagaries of fashion. Take two examples, the long sword and the mail shirt, both of Celtic antecedents. What we see if we trace the development of the doubled-edged long sword are changes in hilt styles and a far greater range of changes in scabbard fittings and suspension methods, but none of the changes as we move from Celtic to Roman to Germanic versions of the weapon fundamentally altered it or improved it. With the possible exception of the move away from all-metal scabbards, this exception occurred quite early in the weapon's history – the rest of the story is one of change as a result of the impact of hinterland fashion on the metropolis, as well as the copying of successful armies by their less successful enemies. What we see with the sword is many respects also true of the mail shirt, particularly its neck closure system. This changes from shoulder-doubling to breastplates to a simple opening, with no system being intrinsically superior. As to the size of the shirt, we see long and short varieties with various sleeve lengths, all as a result of changing influences, and this is as true for the Viking period as for the Roman and Anglo-Saxon periods.

If we now turn to the subject at hand, namely Viking military equipment, with particular reference to the wars with Anglo-Saxon England, matters are not as clear-cut as we might like. In order to build a coherent picture, we have to study both Anglo-Saxon and Viking artefacts. The reason for this is straightforward: the success of the Vikings meant that their equipment was copied. While we can say that an object such as a sword or shield boss is Viking in style because of its date and because we can compare it with finds from known Viking sites across not only the period, but also from across the Viking world as a whole, we cannot always say it was owned by a Viking. It is also important to stress that, in respect of Anglo-Saxon England, the wealth of the period from an English point of view is not so much archaeological as representational and literary. Thus, the fact that we see the same artefacts used by both the Vikings and the English allows us to use the wealth of representational evidence, in sculpture and in manuscripts, to build a convincing picture of the range of artefacts that were in use.

Therefore when we look firstly at armour and then at arms, the fact that both sides are essentially using the same pieces of equipment means that we are surveying not simply Viking but also Anglo-Saxon military equipment. Certainly, if we compare Merovingian-period finds from Norway and Finland with finds from the same period in England we see a commonality of style and therefore of interconnecting influences around the whole of the North Sea. It is thus unsurprising that this continues into the Viking period, particularly when one remembers the perceived success of the Vikings themselves. To draw a parallel, French military dress styles were copied and emulated up until the debacle of the Franco-Prussian War; after that Prussian style was in vogue.

ARMOUR

In the literature of the day we find that according to *Maxims I*, '… to the bold [belongs] a helmet …', while *Maxims II* states that '… blade must strive with helmet in battle …' In *Beowulf* and the *Fight at Finnsburg* the armoured warrior is a recurring leitmotif, yet in the *Battle of Maldon* armour is barely mentioned. Armour also appears on the Franks Casket, the Repton Stone, a fragment of a frieze from Winchester, in manuscript illustrations, and of course on the Bayeux Tapestry. As to the archaeology, we have four helmets and one set of mail from England for the whole of the Anglo-Saxon period. Leaving aside the finds from Vendel and Valsgärde, we have only one complete Viking helmet. However, to put the archaeology (and possibly the whole question of armour provision) in context, we must consider the size of the Imperial Roman Army in the mid-second century AD. There is of course no definite answer to the question of how big the Roman army was: we are dealing with people's best estimates based upon the available evidence. Thus, Brian Dobson has arrived at 384,000 (157,000 legionaries and 227,000 auxilia), while Anthony Birley has argued for 415–445,000 men (in the mid-160s AD). Even if we take the lower figure, and bearing in mind the unarmoured slingers and Numidian cavalry depicted on Trajan's Column, we are

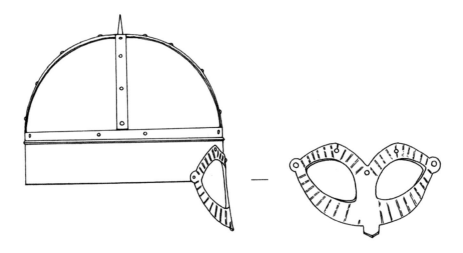

The Gjermundbu helmet. (Redrawn by M. Daniels from Grieg 1947)

still looking at well over 300,000 armoured infantry and cavalry. Today, if we brought together every single surviving Roman helmet, not just for the second century AD but from the period of the Punic Wars to the Islamic Conquest, we would be very lucky to have enough helmets to outfit a single legion (approximately 5,000 men). In this light, the lack of armour in the archaeological record is put more into perspective.

As to the types of armour used by the Vikings and their enemies, we must consider helmets, shields and body armour. Other armour, specifically greaves and vambraces, may also have been used; however, the evidence for their use, particularly in the West, is circumstantial in the extreme. The East is, however, another matter. This does not mean that we will not be considering other armour for, particularly given the crossover which occurred, it would be unwise to categorically rule out the use of items of armour such as greaves and vambraces, as well as weapons such as the mace. However, as we shall see, while some Eastern fashions became universal, others did not and their appearance in Viking Age England would have been both rare and probably unusual.

There exists, to date, only a single practically complete Viking helmet find. Specifically, a helmet from a Scandinavian context which is later than the Vendel period and yet which pre-dates the tenth-century military equipment revolution. The find in question is the late ninth- or early tenth-century Gjermundbu helmet. Gjermundbu, certainly when compared to the finds from the Vendel and Valsgärde boat graves, was a very plain and simple object. The helmet consisted of a simple round iron cap, with narrow crest and lateral bands and a small spike at the apex. The brow band was relatively broad, the eyes and nose of the wearer were protected with spectacles, while mail guarded the neck. Given the level of settlement and trade that took place during and as a result of the first Viking age, it is highly likely that Gjermundbu-type helmets were imported into and used not only in the Danelaw but throughout the whole of Anglo-Saxon England.

Alongside the Gjermundbu helmet, we also see from Anglo-Viking sculpture the use by both sides of what could be called *English*-style helmets. The four helmets from Anglo-Saxon England – Sutton Hoo, Coppergate, Benty Grange and Pioneer – break down into two types. The first type, which can be described as Romano-Swedish, contains but one example: the helmet from mound 1 at Sutton Hoo. The second type, the English or Anglo-Saxon type, contains the remaining three helmets which, although individually different, are enough alike in basics to show a family connection.

The helmet from mound 1 at Sutton Hoo has features in common with both Late Roman ridge helmets and the helmet finds from Vendel and Valsgärde in Sweden, although this is hardly surprising given the fact that the Swedish finds were undoubtedly influenced in their design by Late Roman military fashion. Compare for example the Deurne helmet with the Sutton Hoo, Valsgärde 8 and Vendel XIV. Nor should we view the Sutton Hoo helmet as a unique find for this country, for potentially similar Romano-Swedish or Vendel-style crested helmets appear on Viking Age sculptures from Sockburn and Brompton.

As for the remaining three helmets – Pioneer, Benty Grange and Coppergate – although, as has already been stated, they are superficially different they do share a number of features which mark them out as having been designed and constructed along similar lines. In all three cases the helmet's basic structure comprises a brow band, a crest band and a lateral band, with plates being used to fill the gaps between the bands. Equally, in all cases the crest band was extended to form a nasal, while the broad brow band was cut away or open at the front to form eyeholes. Artistically similar helmets appear, in an Anglian context, on the Franks Casket and the Aberlemno Stone.

It thus appears that during the first Viking age a range of helmet types were both available to and used by both sides in the conflict that swept across the English nations. Yet for all this wealth of variety (and the use of spangenhelme and lamellar helmets alongside the helmet types discussed above is also a distinct possibility), it appears that such styles as were popular and common prior to the tenth century did not survive into that century. For in the tenth century we see a military equipment revolution. However, having said that, this tenth-century revolution is probably best compared to the Imperial Roman Army's Antonine equipment revolution of the second century AD, in that it was a change in fashion and form rather than a change in function.

The new helmet style which swept Western Europe in the tenth century was not really that new; rather it was the latest version of that old classic the conical helmet. Conical helmets appear in Assyrian art, on Parthian coins and in use by the Imperial Roman Army. Why this style has proved popular is best explained by examining the variants, both ancient and modern, of this design. Modern examples of the conical helmet are the 'Mitre' cap, the shako, the busby and the bearskin.

While it remains true that all of the examples given above, be it Napoleonic shako or Assyrian helmet, provided a crumple zone, this extra protective feature was merely a by-product of the head-gear's display function. For all tall headgear was designed to impress, intimidate and overawe an opponent by the simple expedient of increasing the wearer's height.

As to the specifics of the new helmets themselves, the archaeological evidence from East-central Europe ties in remarkably well with the representational evidence from this country. The Eastern European evidence, which is itself merely a reflection of contemporary steppe fashion, is an example of hinterland *élan* in

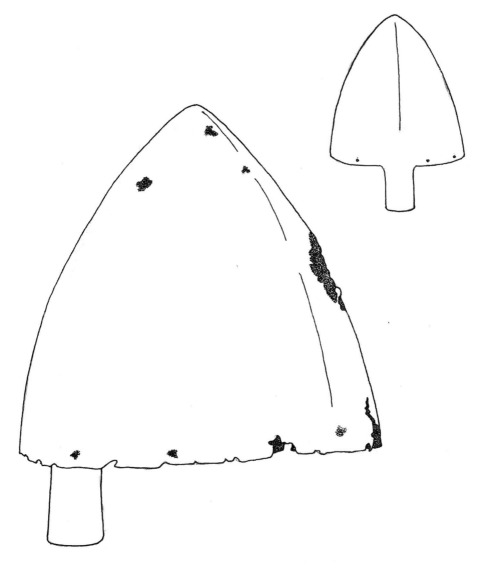

The eleventh-century Olmutz helmet – archetypal of the new fashion which swept Western Europe. (Redrawn by M. Daniels from Nicolle 1988)

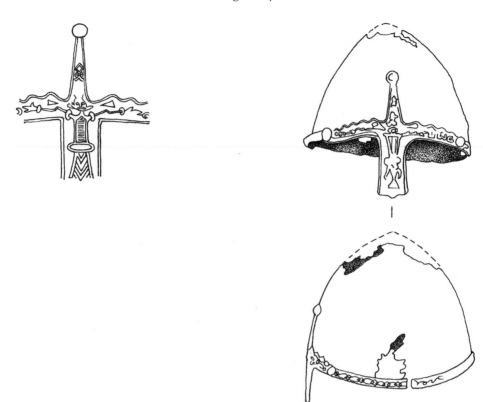

The St Wenceslaus helmet. (Redrawn by M. Daniels from Nicolle 1988)

the medieval world. Thus finds of simple helmets formed from a single piece of iron without a nasal, such as the Hradsko, Bohemia, find; or with an integral nasal, such as the Olmütz, Moravia, find; or with a separate, attached nasal, such as the St Wenceslas helmet in Prague appear on the Bayeux Tapestry, and in British Library manuscripts Cotton Cleopatra C VIII, Cotton Claudius B IV, Harley 603, and on a coin (dated 1053–6) of Edward the Confessor. Segmented helmets, such as a poorly provenanced example in the Metropolitan Museum of Art, New York, and a gilded Polish helmet, currently on loan to the Royal Armouries from Liverpool Museum, appear on the head of Goliath in British Library MS Cotton Tiberius C VI, and of course on the Bayeux Tapestry. More importantly for us, conical helmets also appear on tenth-century Viking sculpture from Middleton and Sockburn.

Cheek pieces on conical helmets, which are known from the twelfth-century Lewis chessmen, do not appear to have been used in this period. Some of the helmets on the Bayeux Tapestry appear to have an extension on the back of the helmet; this may represent a neck guard. Equally, illustrations of conical helmets which both pre- and post-date the Tapestry show such helmets with decorative and/or identification (the purpose is uncertain) ribbons hanging from the back of the helmets in much the same place as these extensions. Thus, the Bayeux Tapestry may be showing us ribbons rather than neck-guards. Where protection for the neck and the side of the face is shown, although none survives archaeologically from this period, it takes the form of either a mail coif or a mail hood which is integral with the body of the hauberk.

Before going on to consider the question of the level of helmet ownership, an aspect of the representational evidence needs to be considered. For with manuscript depictions of headgear we are at times defeated by the simplicity of the illustrations. Thus we need to ask, is what is being shown a hat, or a helmet, or a helmet covered by some form of decorative covering?

The mounted army depicted in the eleventh-century British Library MS Cotton Claudius B IV in many ways typifies the problem as a whole – what do the various cone-shaped pieces of headgear worn by the riders represent? It is of course entirely possible that they simply represent hats made from either cloth or leather. Leather helmets are easily dismissed as a fiction without evidence. Decorative helmet covers, although a feature of the Byzantine and Islamic worlds, do not appear to have been a feature of North-West European warfare and can thus be discounted. The final possibility is that all of the warriors are helmeted, and this is not as far-fetched a possibility as it may seem. The straight cones in the manuscript illustration represent simple conical helmets. Unequivocal depictions of conical helmets with forward-pointing peaks are known from both contemporaneous and earlier Carolingian manuscripts, and these may also provide an explanation for the cone headgear with forward pointing peaks in MS Cotton Claudius B IV and other late Anglo-Saxon manuscripts. Finally, the rumpled cone shapes. Although usually interpreted as folds of cloth, they could equally represent fluted helmets. Generally viewed as a later Western style, flute helmets are known from both Carolingian and post-Carolingian illustrations and certainly existed in the Islamic world by the eleventh century at the latest.

How common were helmets?

> 1008. Here the king [Æthelred] ordered that they should determinedly build ships all over England: that is, one warship from three hundred and 10 hides, and from 8 hides a helmet and mailcoat.
>
> Anglo-Saxon Chronicle E manuscript

Brooks argues that the Anglo-Saxon Chronicle entry for 1008 saw the English finally become comparable, in equipment terms, with their continental counterparts, which from a Viking point of view could be used to suggest that helmets were more common among the Vikings than with their English 'victims'. Certainly the chronicle entry, combined with the *heriots* and the surviving wills of the same period, seems to point to a great deal of deal of armour, albeit post-AD 1008, at least in an English context. Universality is, however, another matter. The representational and literary sources, supported by the evidence of *heriots*, point

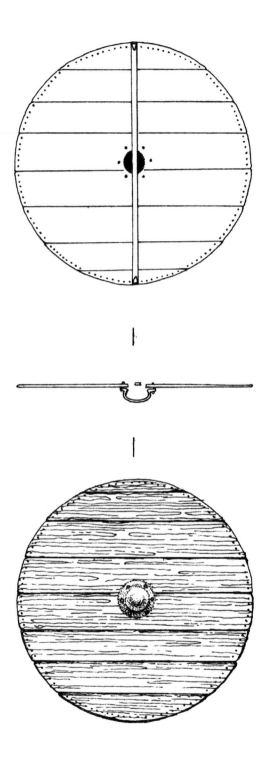

A shield from the Gokstad ship. (Redrawn by M. Daniels from Nicolaysen 1882)

to different levels of provision dependant upon status, and indeed this conclusion is borne out by comparison with Carolingian capitularies.

In answer to the question – how common were helmets? – helmets were probably far more common than was body armour. Indeed, if one considers armour provision and the history of close-order infantry combat from its beginnings in Classical Greece up to AD 1066 (leaving to one side the armour high point of the Imperial Roman Army in the first and second centuries AD) then the general pattern was for the provision of at least a helmet and a shield, with a part of the army having helmet, shield and body armour. It is to this minimum standard (helmet and shield, with some helmet, shield and body armour) that all armies, Viking, English and Frankish, aspired. It may well be that the wealth of the late Anglo-Saxon state allowed this standard to be exceeded, with a greater proportion of body armoured men to non-body armoured men, and this may well explain the entry for 1008 in the E ms. of the Anglo-Saxon Chronicle and its supporting evidence. As to the question of the Vikings and the level of body armour, we will return to that in due course.

The shield in the northern world in the early medieval period shows evidence of both continuity and change: continuity in that the large, flat circular shield of the Migration period continued in use through until the Battle of Hastings; change in that by 1066 it had mostly been replaced by the kite shield.

The *early* shield, the shield of the Migration period and the first Viking wars, continued remarkably unchanged into the second Viking period. Indeed, why should it not? The design itself had remained unchanged from at least the third century AD, if not earlier. In basic terms the shield consisted of a large (diameter 84–118 cm) circular, flat or slightly convex (in one plane only) wooden board. Although the Viking-period Gokstad ship finds show that the board need not be covered, generally a leather covering on either the front, or the rear, or on both sides of the shield board was employed. The shield was edged with either a metal or leather rim, which was sewn in place. The shield was held by a single central grip, the hand being protected by a metal shield boss, and it is in this metal shield boss that we potentially see the only real break with the past.

When we consider pre-Viking shield boss forms, we see similar carinated styles in Scandinavia as across the rest of North-Western Europe. Moving into the Viking period, while at times slight carination continued, as evidenced by the finds from Dublin and L'Ile de Groix, in the main we see hemispherical bosses, typified by the finds from Gokstad and Birka, but also again L'Ile de Groix. Alongside that most Viking of styles, the hemisphere, we also find conical boss styles. Such bosses occur archaeologically in Scotland, the Isles and Norway. Moving into the Second Viking Age we are, as with helmets, left in a position where we have to interpret representational evidence in the light of earlier finds and contemporaneous parallels, for from the evidence of the surviving manuscript illustrations it appears that the earlier styles of shield boss were replaced by the conical form. For the Anglo-Saxons, it is of course entirely possible that the lack of continuity is more imagined than real. That scribal simplicity, in the case of a minor artefact such as the shield boss, has glossed over the continued use of the sugar-loaf shield boss (Evison types e and f) into the late Anglo-Saxon period. Equally, however, given that conical and sub-conical forms are known from tenth- and eleventh-century Scandinavian and Byzantine contexts, and given the ease of transmission of military equipment forms from east to west, it seems likely that even if sugar-loaf bosses continued in use by the Vikings as well as the English, they co-existed alongside other more typical Viking forms. It is also likely that the more common, archaeologically at least, Viking domed shield boss (see, for example, the finds from the Gokstad ship) was not wholly displaced and continued in use into the second Viking age.

The kite shield is yet another example of the fact that Anglo-Saxon/Anglo-Danish England, indeed Western Europe as a whole, was not some isolated military pocket; rather, it was connected to and influenced by the peoples of the steppes, the Islamic world, and Byzantium. The adoption of the kite shield in the eleventh century and the conical helmet in the tenth shows that the Vikings in England were a part of the mainstream of European military culture.

The dominance of the kite shield over other forms is demonstrated by its ubiquity on the Bayeux Tapestry. The reasons behind its rise are, as will be seen, also understandable; its origins are, however, harder to ascertain. The kite shield appeared first in the Byzantine and Islamic worlds, although given our current state of knowledge, it is impossible to state where it was first developed or if we are looking at a case of simultaneous development. The Byzantine *Sylloge tacticorum* (38.1), which dates to c. AD 950, describes Byzantine infantry shields which were broad at the top and narrow at the bottom – kite-shaped in fact. Even here, though, the Byzantines may not have been the originators of the design, in that it may have been adapted from an Iranian infantry shield. Alternatively, it may have first appeared in Umayyad Andalus. A fragment of painted stucco found in the ruins of the Moorish palace at Madina-al-Zahra near Cordoba in Spain and dated to the tenth century shows an armoured cavalryman with a large kite shield.

If the origins of the kite shield are obscure then the same cannot be said for the reasons behind the rapidity of its adoption beyond its first home, nor its continued popularity. It continued in this, its early form, until c. 1150–1200; from this date on it became more triangular in shape and this large triangular shield continued to be used until c. 1250, at which point we see more evolution.

No extant examples survive from this period. However, it is possible to attempt, based upon the representational evidence and later surviving examples, a reconstruction, in the course of which the reasons behind the popularity of the shield will become apparent.

Kite shields, in this period, appear to have been approximately 60 cm wide at their widest point and 120 cm long. They were in all probability constructed from planks and covered with leather. In terms of thickness, a late twelfth-century example in the Swiss National Museum in Zurich was made from wood 15 mm thick. The Swiss example was covered in parchment, which may also have been used in the period under discussion. Certainly, in terms of thickness this is greater than earlier Anglo-Saxon shields, which by the seventh century only averaged 8.5 mm. Indeed, it is also thicker than Imperial Roman plank shields, which show thicknesses similar to the early English examples. Kite shields were either flat (they are shown being used as a table on the Bayeux Tapestry) or slightly convex in the horizontal plane (as is shown in the *c.* 1140–50 'Temple Pyx'). Anything other than slightly convex can be discounted, as this would make them unusable on horseback. Rims are definitely apparent from the representational evidence, and were probably most commonly made of leather (possibly *cuir bouilli* or rawhide), although metal rims cannot be discounted. The rim was probably held in place by sewing or, in the case of a metal rim, sewing and clips.

Despite depictions of shield bosses on kite shields on the Bayeux Tapestry, the shield was not held solely in one hand. The bosses shown on the Bayeux Tapestry and on other depictions of the kite shield were decorative, although they may have served a limited offensive function. Equally, those shields on the Bayeux Tapestry which appear to have simply a single strap on the rear should be ignored as a simplification of the true picture. Rather, the shield was held (on the left arm) using a series of leather straps (brases or enarmes) which formed a combined arm and handgrip (similar in concept to the grip arrangement on the Greek *hoplon*). The forearm rested against an oblong pad. A shoulder or neck strap (a guige) was also fitted; this strap was probably adjustable.

The kite shield, when compared to its predecessor the circular shield, was a large shield – it was longer, thicker and heavier, yet we should not see it as unwieldy. Nor should we view it as better; rather, we should view it in its context. For a horse-riding warrior aristocracy who were expected to be able to fight on both foot and horse (and possibly more on horseback than was previously the norm) and certainly from a continental viewpoint with the rise of the crossbow, it was ideally suited to the tactical circumstances of the day. On horseback it protected the whole of the rider's left side; on foot in the shieldwall it offered protection to the vulnerable lower left leg. The increased thickness and thus weight was compensated for by the new carrying mechanism and was designed to give the defence an edge over the attack.

It has been argued that the Vikings' success, particularly at the beginning of the second Viking age, can be attributed to their greater use of body armour, especially when compared to their English opponents. The strength of this argument is based upon the single possible mention of English armour in the poem *The Battle of Maldon* and the Anglo-Saxon Chronicle entry for AD 1008.

> Then an armed man approached the earl; he wanted to acquire that warrior's armrings, *reaf and gold bands, and the ornamented sword.*
>
> *The Battle of Maldon*, lines 159–161

Reaf means, according to Clark Hall's *A Concise Anglo-Saxon Dictionary*, 'plunder, booty, spoil, garment, armour, vestment.' Scragg, in his *The Battle of*

Maldon, translates it as robe (or garment); others, but by no means all, have preferred the 'armour' meaning of the word. How this word has been understood, for it is the only possible mention of the use of armour by the English in the whole poem, has affected people's understanding of the warfare of the period.

Halsall, while accepting that metal helmets and armour could have been easily produced in the early medieval west, argues that from the 950s English armies engaged in mobile warfare against the Welsh and the Scots may have discarded their armour. Brooks, arguing that the English at Maldon in AD 991 were unarmoured, sees them as inadequately equipped, unable to fight at close quarters and reluctant and unable to stand against an enemy superior in equipment terms.

In the summer of 168 BC, at Pydna in Greece, in a short, hard-fought, bloody fight at close-quarters, the armoured might of Rome crushed Macedon. According to Polybius (XXIX.17):

> Aemilius the consul, who had never seen a phalanx until this occasion in the war with Perseus, often confessed afterwards to certain persons in Rome that he had never seen anything more terrible and dreadful than a Macedonian phalanx, and this although he had witnessed and directed as many battles as any man.

And the most terrible part of that dreadful army? According to Plutarch it was the Theban contingent, who were armoured solely with shield and greaves. During the principate of Domitian, at Mons Graupius in Scotland, armoured Imperial Roman auxiliary infantry attacked uphill, slaughtering their barbarian opponents (Tacitus, *Agricola*, 36). Armour was not a bar to movement, nor did it prevent the wearer fighting in raiding and skirmish warfare; the Anglo-Scottish Border Reivers, it must be remembered, were armoured. Neither did the lack of it prevent close-order infantry combat. Nor was its presence (or absence for that matter) the reason for the English defeat at Maldon.

The armoured warrior was an Early Medieval leitmotif; he appears in *Beowulf*, *The Fight at Finnsburg*, in *Judith*, in *Andreas* and in *Elene*, on the Franks Casket, the Repton Stone, on a fragment of a frieze from Winchester, in numerous manuscript illustrations and of course on the Bayeux Tapestry. Body armour formed a part of the artistic milieu of the aristocracy; equally, it formed a very real part of their material culture. For English armies were a part of the mainstream of European military culture (witness the swift adoption of conical helmets and kite shields) and thus little different from their European counterparts, and they were generally well armoured. There is no real reason, nor evidence, to support the hypothesis that armour was either absent from, or temporarily abandoned by, English armies in the late Anglo-Saxon period. Thus at Maldon, or rather in the poem, *reaf* is probably best translated as armour; indeed, given Byrhtnoth's position and status it is highly unlikely that he went to battle unarmoured.

How then should we view the Anglo-Saxon Chronicle E manuscript entry for 1008, and the appearance at around the same time of armour in *heriots*? Certainly not as a sudden rush to introduce armour in order to achieve parity with an enemy superior in equipment. Rather, we should see it as an attempt to bring the nation's wealth into play in order to increase and formalise the provision of an existing resource. For the protective effect of armour is both individual and cumulative. A line (or lines) of armoured men, in close order, have a tactical advantage over a similar unarmoured formation, in that they are harder to kill. The Romans had the resources to equip whole units, indeed whole armies, with metal body armour. The late Anglo-Saxon state, although doubtless aware of the cumulative value of armour, was not able to do as much as Imperial Rome. It was, however, probably the most centralised, organised state in Europe at that time, with a competent revenue-raising system and an efficient administration. Thus we should see the late Anglo-Saxon state attempting to provide, if not necessarily whole armies of armoured warriors, at least ranks of them. Where then does this leave the Vikings?

The Vikings were no different in respect of armour provision than their enemies, about whom we are better blessed for evidence. The upper echelons of society, as in all such martial societies, were better equipped than those who, although weapons-worthy, were lower down the social ladder. All may have strove to be fully equipped with a panoply of bright wargear which included body armour. However, this was not possible. The Imperial Roman armies of the first and second centuries after the birth of Christ set the high-water mark for armour provision. The Vikings could not emulate this. Instead, they inhabited a world where armour was common but far from universal. Like all early medieval forces, for the Vikings armour went with social status. It will have trickled down from the elite to the ranks of their armed retainers, but exactly how common it was is impossible to say. At best, it was probably more common than we are at times willing to concede, while still being a long way from the level of provision we associate with Rome.

The predominant form of body armour was mail, and it appears to have come in a variety of styles. Archaeologically, the seventh-century mail shirt from mound I at Sutton Hoo seems to have been long-sleeved and knee-length, while the fourth- or fifth-century Vimose and the eighth- to eleventh-century Vaerdalen, North Trondelag and Romel, Melhus, South Trondelag (although not completely intact) mail shirts appear to have been at least hip-length with elbow-length sleeves. The mail from the Gjermundbu find is, sadly, fragmentary. In all save one case, prior to the adoption of the hooded ventail form, all the evidence points to a simple wide-necked cuirass. The exception is two figures engaged in combat in British Library MS Cotton Cleopatra C VIII. Here the two warriors, who are both wearing short-sleeved, waist-length mail, have very tight neck closure, which appears to have been facilitated by a short closed slit at the front of the neck. How this worked in practice, if it is not scribal error, is unknown. There is no evidence for the hooks or breastplates of the Roman period.

The representational evidence is both more detailed and, with the potential for scribal error mentioned above, more open to flaws. Thus we see waist-length mail with short sleeves in British Library MS Cotton Cleopatra C VIII;

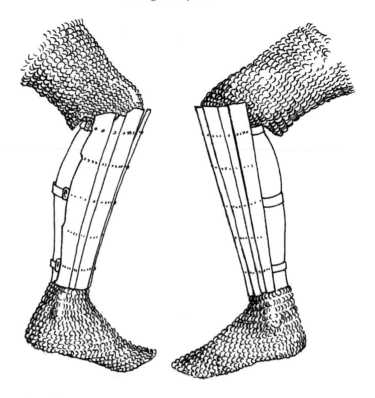

The greaves from Valsgärde 8. (Redrawn by M. Daniels from Cedelof 1973)

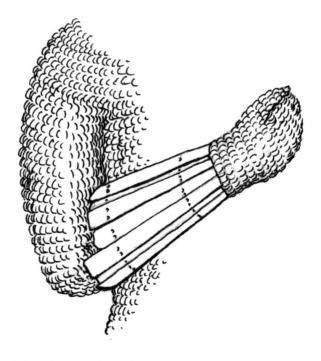

The vambrace from Valsgärde 8. (Redrawn by M. Daniels from Cedelof 1973)

knee-length mail, split front and back, with short or elbow-length sleeves in British Library MS Cotton Claudius B IV; knee-length mail, split front and back, with three-quarter-length sleeves in British Library MS Harley 603; knee-length mail (this is what the apparent shorts most probably represent), split front and back, with three-quarter-length sleeves, integral hood and ventail in the Bayeux Tapestry. The picture is thus one of diversity as opposed to uniformity.

The edged square seen on some mail shirts on the Bayeux Tapestry is probably best interpreted as a ventail, an integral flap of mail designed to protect the mouth and lower face which was tied in place. A re-enforcing square of mail on the chest would not require the leather edging it is depicted as having, whereas a ventail would. Indeed, it also appears that as well as edging the ventail, the leather (the leather is supposition, but it is a likely supposition) also held in place a lining, such as the one shown in the Hrabanus Maurus manuscript at Monte Cassino. Mail which had a slight hole to allow the sword hilt to pass through, and where the body of the sword was worn and suspended beneath the armour, appears from the Bayeux Tapestry to have been more of a Norman, as opposed to an Anglo-Danish, fashion, although the style would not have been unknown in this country.

Besides mail, the possibility exists that lamellar was also worn. Finds from the Viking site of Birka, in Sweden, have been dated to AD 900–950. The Birka finds, which appear to be of Old Turkic origin, were probably obtained either via the Rus or from Byzantium. Lamellar, even in the Roman Period, was never a popular form of armour in the West, yet finds such as those from Birka, from Charavines in Provence, Niederstotzingen, and of course Wisby, along with the Isola Rizza dish and a ninth-century Carolingian ivory in the cathedral treasury in Nancy, show that lamellar was worn in Western Europe, even if only in a limited manner, from the end of the Roman Period through until the fourteenth century. It is thus possible that it was also used, again to a limited extent, by some Vikings in England.

Limb defences, greaves and vambraces, may also have had a limited currency in the Viking Age in the West. We of course have the earlier Valsgärde finds, in the form of the splint greaves and vambrace from Valsgärde 8. There is also Byzantine evidence and, although this is hardly surprising, it does open up a Rus connection. Such armour is mentioned in Carolingian written sources which, while not entirely clear, do suggest the use of splint armour. Earlier Greek and Roman greaves were one- or, at most, two-piece constructions. Splint construction is an easier and not an inferior substitute for earlier types. There is, as we can see, a range of examples from across the early medieval period, all of which can be connected to the Vikings. Whether or not all this adds up to their use by those Vikings who attacked the English is another matter. At best it, like lamellar armour, remains a possibility.

Finally, before turning to the subject of weapons, we must consider under-armour padding. Despite the lack of direct evidence for its use, armour does not work properly without it and it was therefore undoubtedly used. In terms of its actual form we must look to earlier evidence, the Roman *thoracomachus*, and later evidence, the medieval *gambeson* and *aketon*. The Roman and medieval versions of under-armour padding were probably very similar in form and thus it is highly likely that the Viking version of the garment was the same as its earlier and later counterparts, namely two layers of linen padded in between with wool and quilted vertically.

WEAPONS

Successful armies are copied – armaments are imitated. Nor should this be viewed as a new process; the Hellenistic armies of the successor states, which were modelled on Philip's great creation, the Macedonian phalanx, were themselves reformed along Roman lines in the 160s BC. The Swiss pike formations were copied to some extent and then employed, albeit with disastrous results, by the Scots at Flodden in 1513. Later we see hussars being copied across Europe, while in the late nineteenth century, as a result of Prussia's success against Austria and France, the pickelhaube replaced the kepi across the world. In the twentieth century, the success of the AK-47 can in part be attributed to the fact that its effectiveness is combined with a simple yet robust design.

It holds true, of course, that merely adopting the latest in military fashion is not always enough and can lead to catastrophic results. We see nothing, however, so dramatic in the military equipment of the early medieval period. In England the events which led to the change in style of Anglo-Saxon military equipment, namely the first Viking age and the unification of England, were dramatic in themselves and the changes that occurred took place along what could be called 'Roman' lines. Roman weapons conformed always to a basic 'fire and shock' pattern and their main forces over time remained close-order infantry. Thus, the changes could be categorised as being more of style than of substance. The English were essentially the same for, with one exception – the broad axe – and that may well have been a response to a new tactical situation, the weapons of the Migration period and the weapons of Hastings differed in aesthetic rather than in practical terms, and that also holds true the Viking weapons.

The catalyst for the aesthetic changes, the final nails in the coffin of the earlier styles, came from the Viking raiders (later armies and settlers) who first appeared in AD 789. The changes that occurred were not only the inevitable result of a new dynamic cultural input, they were also unsurprising. Unsurprising in that we see changes in style and appearance prior to the first Viking age and there is thus every reason to believe that change would have occurred and continued to occur even without the Vikings – they merely added to the mix. Inevitable for the English – well, we are back to the copying of successful armies. For the Vikings, we see change as part of an ongoing process over time. Equally, the similarity of the weapons styles in Scandinavia in the pre-Viking age to Germanic Europe show that it was the perceived military success of the Vikings which can account for the spread of Viking-style sword pommels and shield bosses. However, given the fact that the new was not so different to the old, we could simply be seeing the acceleration of an existing cultural dynamic.

Bone, in his 1989 paper 'The Development of Anglo-Saxon Swords from the Fifth to the Eleventh Century', notes that in general terms English swords varied little, in terms of their overall dimensions, over the period as a whole. These dimensions were an overall length of 81–97 cm, a blade length of 68–81 cm, and blade width (at the lower guard) of 4.5–6.5 cm. However, if we look at Geibig's classification of Viking sword blades we see a slightly different picture. Geibig's Type 5 (blade length 84–91 cm, blade width 4.8–5.1 cm), which was in use from the mid-tenth through to the mid- to late eleventh century, was slightly longer than Bone's general analysis, while his Type 4 (which was in use at roughly the same time as the Type 5) was a smaller weapon, with a blade length of 63–76 cm and a blade width of 4.5–5.0 cm. Thus, Bone's statement, while essentially true, needs qualifying with respect to Geibig and as a result we should therefore expect that both sides, in the period under study, fought with a greater range of swords (in terms of size) than was previously supposed.

Viking swords, particularly the hilts, have been long and extensively studied. As a result, the subject has accrued a respectable corpus. The foundation text is Petersen's 1919 *De Norske Vikingesverd*. The main English works on the subject are Wheeler's 1927 catalogue for the Museum of London entitled *London and the Vikings*, Oakeshott's 1960 *The Archaeology of Weapons*, and most recently Peirce's 2002 *Swords of the Viking Age*, all of which build on Petersen's work. It is with the hilt that we see the greatest changes and the defining stylistic break between pre-Viking and Viking swords. We thus see pommels and guards wholly of iron, although there was the odd exception in material (we sometimes find, as in the example from York, bone, including whalebone, being used). In terms of style, what we are seeing is a change in construction from the sandwich hilt fittings we see in Norway and the rest of Scandinavia prior to the Viking Age to solid, usually iron, hilt fittings. In terms of shape and appearance the earlier forms are obvious direct ancestors of the later, yet why the change in material and construction? It has been argued that the change came about in order to balance the larger and heavier blades which were coming into fashion from *c*. AD 800. This may well be the case, although the range of blade sizes makes this broad argument not universally applicable. Possibly we are seeing Steppe influence, but this would be more likely later in the period, after the Vikings had had far more contact with the peoples of the Steppe and, of course, with Byzantium, although this was not a closed world and some influence is still possible. The first explanation is most probably correct; certainly, of the reconstructions I have seen of both Viking and pre-Viking swords, the iron hilts of the Viking period have balanced the blade better and would have given the warrior a greater degree of control.

Scabbards rarely survive in the archaeological record. From the Viking period, scabbards, with the exception of fragments adhering to blades, do not survive at all. However, such evidence as we do have, combined with appropriate parallels (from Germanic bog finds and from the Roman world), allows us to accurately reconstruct the structure of the scabbard. Two thin pieces of wood surrounded the blade; although plain wooden examples are known, albeit from the Nydam find, generally the outside of the scabbard was covered with leather or cloth. A greased or oiled internal lining, again of cloth or leather, but also at times of fur, was present in order to protect the sword blade. Such a lining helped to hold the sword firmly in the scabbard, yet it did not impede drawing. Decorative chapes and scabbard mouths appear to have been used throughout the period; see, for example, the late eleventh-century carving at Ebberston Church near Scarborough. Their use does not, however, appear to have been universal, and they are absent from the Bayeux Tapestry. In all cases the scabbard should be viewed as a thing of beauty, a means by which images of martial terror, and personal wealth, could be projected. Indeed, if we consider feudal Japan, it should be noted that while their sword blades are merely beautiful, their scabbards are exquisite.

Our understanding of sword suspension in this period is problematic to say the least. Cameron, in her work on sheaths and scabbards, appears to have identified indentations which may have been created by scabbard slides on a number of leather scabbard covers from York and Gloucester. Following the fall of the Roman Empire in the West, scabbard slides lost their pre-eminent position; thus, we also see the use of scabbard bosses or buttons (such as in the case of the sword from mound 1 at Sutton Hoo) and a form of ring suspension from the Viking graves at Ballateare and Cronk Moar. Whether all of these systems continued in use throughout the Viking period is hard to ascertain, as such evidence as we have is representational and simplistic in the extreme. The Winchester fragment probably shows a crossed leather strap; the Bayeux Tapestry in the main shows a single line which appears to be a part of the sword belt, although on one occasion the tapestry shows two parallel horizontal bands and on another a double buckled sword belt. British Library MS Cotton Tiberius C VI's Goliath has a decorated baldric which wraps once around the scabbard. Whether you use a sword belt or a baldric, and both appear to have been used, the fact remains that it must be held securely in place and at present the current state of the evidence does not allow us to say how this was done. However, it is possible that in the surviving art we are seeing the beginnings of the elaborate thonging and lacing which secured the sword belt to the scabbard in the post-1066 medieval world.

While generally viewed as more of a Continental weapon, the *seax* was in Scandinavia, as with Anglo-Saxon England, little used, or so the archaeological evidence would suggest. It may be that as it was more a hunting tool, a thing of the kill, and as such it was not always seen as worthy of burial. Finds dating from the fifth to the seventh centuries from Fjelberg, Holum and Kvam, to name but a few sites in Norway, show that it was carried. Generally, these early examples were up to 25 cm in blade length (the Holum example was unusual in having a blade length of 53 cm), while a contemporary find from Time, also in Norway, had a blade length of 61 cm. Certainly, of these two forms we can see in the longer examples the antecedents of the Viking-age sword *seax*. However, the short *seax* poses a different problem, namely was it used in combat? That the *seax* was carried into battle is not

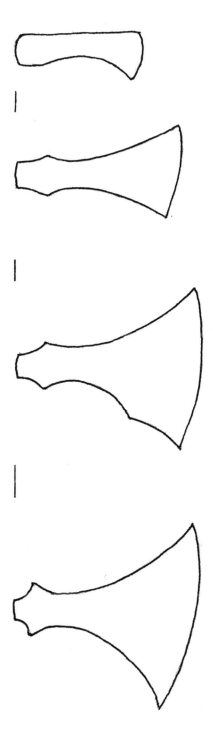

Tenth- and eleventh-century Viking axes. From top to bottom, Wheeler Type I, IV, V & VI. (Redrawn by M. Daniels from Wheeler 1927)

in doubt; whether it was used, or rather whether one form of the object was used in combat, is. Of the two forms of the *seax* that are known from the Viking period, one, the long or sword *seax*, is easily dealt with. Viking examples had 80–90 cm blade lengths; their English counterparts were still between 54 and 76 cm long in terms of blade length and thus perfectly adequate as mêlée weapons. Late Viking single-edged swords with Petersen Type X hilts have been found, and while it is possible that English long *seaxes* may have been fitted with sword hilts, it is equally possible that they had simple hilts or grips without guard or pommel. The shorter English long *seax* would have been suspended horizontally at the waist, as is shown on the Repton Stone, whereas those at the other end of the blade length spectrum would have been worn as a sword on the left hip. It is also probable, as both the Continental evidence and the more native Repton Stone show, that the long *seax* was at times carried alongside, and tertiary to, the spear and the sword.

The short or common seax was effectively a large knife (blade length 8–36 cm), whose milieu was most probably the hunt. It was carried into battle and is shown on sculpture (see, for example, the Viking Middleton warriors and the Repton Stone) purely as a sign of status. In combat it was definitely peripheral, a weapon

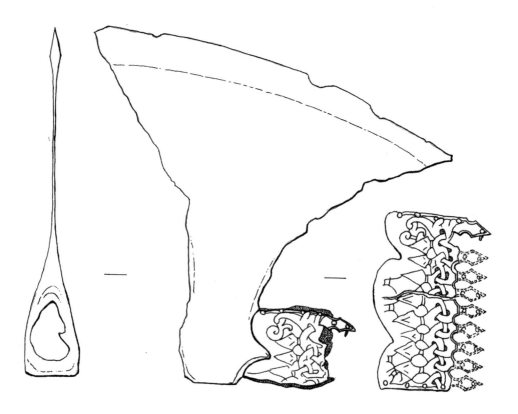

A broad axe with an ornamental socket from Old London Bridge. (Redrawn by M. Daniels from Wheeler 1927)

of last resort. Beowulf is forced to use his 'slaughter-*seax*' because his sword has broken (*Beowulf* lines 2680–7, 2702–4 and 2904). The use of the word 'slaughter' to describe Beowulf's *seax* should not lead us to believe that it was actually an effective close-combat weapon – rather, it describes its function, namely to dispatch, or as the poem puts it, to 'slaughter', wounded animals in the hunt and wounded enemies on the field of battle.

Bradbury's view, expounded in his work *The Battle of Hastings*, that the axe was a 'somewhat antique weapon' and thus the Anglo-Danish use of it was somewhat quaint and outdated is rather far from the truth. The axe, if anything, was in the flower of its manhood. For in England the axe was viewed as an effective cavalry weapon up until the mid-seventeenth century, and it was used by the navy as a close-quarters weapon right through to the early nineteenth century.

William of Poitiers tells us that at Hastings Harold's Anglo-Danish force threw 'murderous axes' and one of the figures on the Bayeux Tapestry does appear to be mirroring William's words. There is, however, no reason to believe that these were the *franciscas* of the Migration period. Instead, we should see them as being axes of Wheeler Types I and IV. A rare late Anglo-Saxon manuscript illustration of an axe in combat, British Library MS Cotton Cleopatra C VIII, may be intended to show either a Wheeler Type IV or V; it could, however, represent the survival of an earlier style in that it resembles the axe-head found in grave 21 at Petersfinger in Wiltshire. The Petersfinger cemetery was in use from the fifth to the seventh century.

Skarp-Hedin came swooping down on him and swung at him with his axe. The axe crashed down on his head and split it down to the jaw-bone, spilling the back-teeth on to the ice.

The Saga of Burnt Njal, 92

Skarp-Hedin and his axe are one of the lasting images from the late thirteenth-century *Njal's Saga*. Indeed, in many ways they are archetypes – Skarp-Hedin is the perfect Viking, arrogant, fearless and axe wielding. As to the type of axe, well he was probably armed with something akin to the Mammen axe, but in the popular imagination it would be the broad or Danish axe that he wielded.

The broad axe (Wheeler Type VI) first appeared around the year 1000 and was still in use, in England at least, as late as 1141, when at the Battle of Lincoln (according to John of Hexham) King Stephen wielded one with such skill and ferocity that he long held his foes at bay. As to the weapon itself, a large (blade length on the curve ranged between approximately 19 and 25 cm) yet surprisingly light head (the weight of a number of examples held in the collection of the Museum of London ranges between 15 oz and 1 lb 11 oz) was attached to a straight wooden shaft approximately five feet in length. The lightness was achieved, as indeed Wheeler notes, by the surprising thinness of the blade, save at the socket and directly behind the edge. In a few cases, decorative copper-alloy

The broad axe in use. An Anglo-Danish housecarl from the Bayeux Tapestry.

tubes lined the inside of the socket and extended someway down the haft. Such tubes should be viewed as decoration, and should not be confused with, nor viewed as an early form of the later medieval langets.

The use of the two-handed broad axe undoubtedly arose from the need to counteract two different tactical situations, one new, the other rather old. The new situation was the increasing use on the Continent of armoured cavalry. The old situation was the need to break the symmetry of shieldwall combat. The appearance of the broad axe around AD 1000 is slightly later, in equipment terms, than the first use of the kite shield and the conical helmet (in many ways the marks of the new armoured knight) and thus this new weapon may well be seen as an infantry response to the increasingly mounted Continental warfare. The tenth-century Byzantine solution, or rather the latest Roman solution, to the problem of stiffening infantry facing an attack by heavy cavalry was the *menavlion*, a long (2.7–3.6 m) heavy spear. The weapon was designed to be thrust two-handed, and was a horse killer. The *menavlion* was in all probability known to the Vikings, yet as a tactical solution it was more fitted to the complex organisation of the Byzantine Army, which was in a position to field whole units of *menavlatoi*. The Vikings needed something less manpower-intensive (something which could possibly be wielded by two or three members of a ship's crew); the solution was the broad axe. Horses will not charge into a solid body of formed infantry; rather they will come to a halt, thus giving the men in the shieldwall an opportunity to distract the rider while the axe-man steps through the rank and kills the horse. How easy this was to achieve in practise is hard to say, although the initial success of Harold at Hastings is worth remembering in this context.

As to its use in the clash of shieldwalls, well, to understand the broad axe's role in that environment, we must turn to the clash of the Swiss and their German counterparts, the Landskechts, during the Renaissance. Tactical symmetry occurs when two similarly equipped and trained armies clash. Such situations are observable in the Hellenistic Period in the wars of the successor states, in the early medieval period in the clash of shieldwalls and in the clash of Renaissance pike formations. Formations, be they shieldwalls or pike blocks, collapse as a result of the creation of tears and gaps which are exploited to literally rip the enemy apart. The problem was how to create the tears and gaps. In the case of Renaissance pike formations the solution arrived at was the *verlorne Haufe* ('lost outfit' or 'forlorn hope'), armed with halberds as well as hand-and-a-half and two-handed swords; advancing ahead of their own pikemen, they would try to hack their way into and so disrupt the enemy's pikes, the resultant confusion caused by the *verlorne Haufe* being, in theory, successfully exploited by their own pikemen. While I am not advocating that English and Viking broad axe-men were some kind of early medieval 'forlorn hope', what I am arguing is that they fulfilled to some extent the same role, namely they attempted to overcome the symmetry by hacking their way into the enemy shieldwall, thus creating a tear or gap which when exploited would lead to the enemy's collapse.

The great two-handed broad axe remains the popular image of the Viking axe, yet it is a relative late-comer, the product of changing tactical circumstances

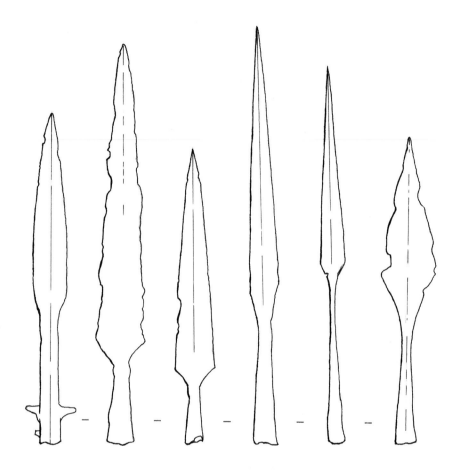

Tenth- and eleventh-century Viking spearheads from England.

which the Vikings did a great deal to provoke and then, in the shape of this new weapon, react to. The axe, as a weapon, has a long history which need not, in the main, concern us here. What we do see is an increase in blade size alongside older forms. Thus, the smaller weapons which we find with the fourth-century Nydam boat continue relatively unchanged until the end of the Viking period (Wheeler Type I). Over time newer, larger variants, Wheeler Types III and IV, arise. The sword was, of course, a prestige and at times highly decorated item; the axe, as the famous Mammen examples show, could equally fulfil the same role.

The mace as a close-combat weapon goes back to prehistory. It is not a weapon that we normally associate with the Vikings. Used in combat on the Eastern frontier of the Roman Empire, its use continued into the Byzantine period. Equally, and for similar reasons, namely the clash of heavily armoured cavalry, it was a steppe weapon. A tenth-century example from Tagantscha gives us a Kievan Rus connection. Whether we can take this Rus connection,

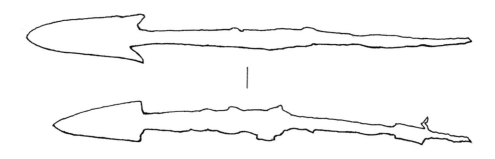

Typical tanged Viking javelin heads.

combined with the Vikings' known association with Byzantium, and translate it to a Western use for the mace is of course another matter. Yes, the spheres overlapped; however, the tactical situations, while at times similar, particularly in relation to European and Byzantine infantry combat, were not identical. The mace, in a Western/Anglo-Saxon context, should therefore be viewed in the same light as lamellar: a distinct possibility, but a novel one, certainly not an everyday one.

The changes which occurred to the sword, and the reasons behind these changes, set the pattern for our understanding of spear type. Turning firstly to the English, despite Brooks' attempt to furnish the English at Maldon with Swanton-type spearheads, it is far more likely that such weapons were those of Byrhtnoth's ancestors than of Byrhtnoth himself. For while it is likely that the English warriors who fought in the first Viking age were armed with 'Swanton' spearheads, it is equally likely that their descendant who fought at Maldon, Ashingdon and Hastings were not.

Instead, we should look to the tenth- and eleventh-century finds from the River Thames. Here, we see both Viking (Petersen Types G, K and M) and Carolingian 'winged' spearheads. The main break with the past in terms of construction was the 'almost universal' (to quote Wheeler) adoption of the closed socket. As for head shapes, angular forms predominated, although 'leaf-bladed' examples, such as the Carolingian 'winged' type, were still used. The change from Swanton's English types to Petersen's Viking types is now largely seen as being a cosmetic one, for there was nothing fundamentally wrong with the earlier English types, nor were the later Viking styles intrinsically better. Yet at the end of the day it comes down to more than the simple question of actual effectiveness. Perceived effectiveness and the copying of successful armies again enter the mix; thus, Viking types replaced Anglo-Saxon types. But apart from that, the spear remained essentially the same. Indeed, it was in its essentials potentially unchanged since the days of Classical Greece. For if we compare head shapes, certainly we lack the range identified by Swanton, but in many respects, other than socket form and the greater preponderance of the 'winged' type, many similarities exist between Viking and Anglo-Saxon spearheads. Thus, we see in Petersen's great work both long and short, leaf and angular bladed spearheads. What we do see is a simplification of cross-section, with the Vikings opting in the main for simple diamond and lenticular forms. Exceptions do of course exist, and both mid-ribbed and fullered examples can still be found, as illustrated by the finds from Rovaniemi and Suomela in Finland.

The reasons for the English adoption of the closed socket are easy to enumerate, the Vikings less so. Partly there does not seem to be a tradition of the split socket in Scandinavia for spearheads, although we do find them on arrowheads. It may be that we are seeing Roman influence, but the question then arises: why did the Anglo-Saxons not adopt this style earlier? The probable explanation is aesthetics. This may seem trite, however the *look of the thing* can play an important part in warfare. The advantage, the aesthetic advantage, the closed socket has over the split is that the former looks better. It is as simple as that. The closed socket has nice, clean lines and because there is no break in the surface, it provides a better medium for decoration.

Finds from the Viking cemetery of Birka point to spear lengths of between 1.8 m and 3.5 m, with the majority being between 2.2 and 2.4 m in length; the Birka finds are very similar to earlier extant examples from Illerup and Nydam, which measured between 2.23 m and 3.54 m, as well as to even earlier Greek and La Tène finds. Earlier Anglo-Saxon finds from Mucking appear to have been between 1.85 m and 2.8 m long. We should therefore expect Viking spears to conform to Birka's 1.8–3.5m range. Questions we have difficulty in answering when it comes to Viking spears relate to the attachment of the head to the shaft, spear shaft decoration and the existence of the butt-spike.

In the case of earlier Roman and Germanic finds (see, for example, the spears from the Nydam bog deposit), both the spearhead and butt-spike were, when attached to the shaft, fitted to a whittled point which was stepped to accommodate the socket and provide a nice clean line. Whether this practice was followed by the Vikings and, for that matter, their Anglo-Saxon opponents, is harder to say. It appears to be shown in the eighth-century Durham Cassiodrus manuscript illustration of David as Victor, and on the spears carried by the Viking-period Sockburn and Middleton warriors, as well as on a metalworker's die from Öland. But in all of these cases we may simply be seeing artistic simplification. Archaeologically, the phenomenon is possibly seen on the spearhead found in grave 55 at the Sewerby inhumation cemetery; even here, however, the practice cannot be confirmed, as the surviving fragment of spearshaft contained within the socket is fragmentary. Thus, stepping may have been practised or it may not – it could well have been a case of personal preference.

1. Vikings! The Lindisfarne Stone. A fragment of a late ninth- or early tenth-century grave marker in the Yorkshire Museum, York.

2. Muscular Christianity. Louis and Charles Rochet's 1882 statue of Charlemagne, Ile de la Cité, Paris.

Above and below: 3. Strategic Mobility 1 – two views of the Skuldelev 5 warship.

4. Strategic Mobility 2 – a reconstruction of a 'dragon' prow in the Wikinger Museum, Haithabu.

5. The River Tyne from the Collingwood Monument, looking towards St Paul's monastery, Jarrow. The monastery was sacked by Vikings in AD 794.

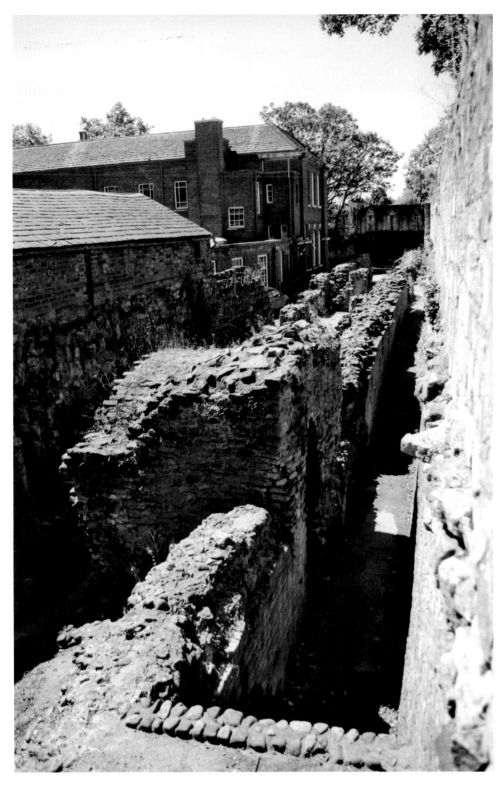

6. The defences of York (1) – the Anglian Tower.

7. The defences of York (2) – the Multangular Tower. Despite its impressive defences, York fell to the Vikings in AD 867.

8. The confluence of the rivers Kennet and Thames. In AD 871, according to Asser, the Vikings fortified a camp between the arms of the two rivers.

9. Portchester, Hampshire. As a late Anglo-Saxon thegnly residence it resumed its former role as a safe harbour from which to combat piracy.

10. The site of the Battle of Maldon in AD 991, with Northey Island and its infamous causeway in the background.

11. Oxford Cathedral and the site of St Frideswide's minster, where a massacre of Danes took place on St Brice's Day 1002.

12. The late tenth-century Danish fortress of Fyrkat. Built during the unification of Denmark, this and similar sites demonstrates the increasing power of the kings of Denmark.

13. A reconstruction of one of the halls which occupied the interior of Fyrkat.

14. A typical Viking shield boss. This example is in the British Museum.

15. The Coppergate helmet. In the Yorkshire Museum, York.

16. A tenth-century Viking warrior cross fragment from Middleton.

17. The Viking-period Brompton Warrior. Of note is the crested Vendel-style helmet.

18. A tenth-century sword from the Thames at Temple, now in the British Museum. The hilt is decorated with animal ornament and the grip is bound with silver wire.

19. The hilt of an eleventh-century sword from the Thames at Battersea, in the Ashmolean Museum.

20. From two different Viking swords we see a whalebone pommel and a bone guard. In the Yorkshire Museum, York.

21. An axe of the second Viking age from York. In the Yorkshire Museum, York.

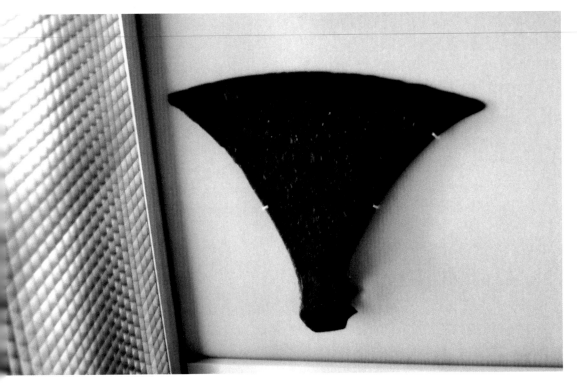

22. A tenth- or eleventh-century broad axe from the Thames, in the British Museum.

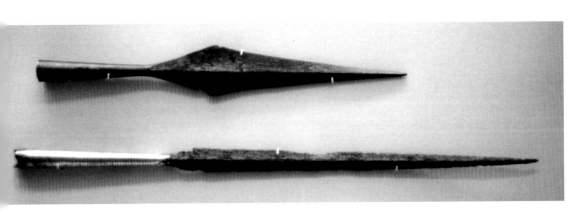

23. Two tenth- or eleventh-century spearheads from the London area, now in the British Museum. Both have decorated sockets; the shorter uses silver inlay, while the longer has twisted silver and copper wires.

24. 'Winged' Carolingian-style spearheads in the British Museum.

25. A part of a Viking saddle and a horse's bit, from York. In the Yorkshire Museum, York.

26. Tenth- or eleventh-century brass-inlaid iron stirrups from Battersea, in the British Museum.

27. A Viking-period spur in the Yorkshire Museum, York.

28. The Ile de la Cité, scene of the siege of AD 885, from the River Seine.

29. The Petit Pont. The modern bridge stands on the site of the bridge attacked by Vikings during the siege of AD 885.

We simply do not know if the Vikings followed the Roman practice of painting their spear-shafts – there is an absence of evidence, thus we unable to either support or refute painting. However, remembering Vegetius' words (*Epitome Rei Militaris* II.14) 'the glitter of arms strikes very great fear in the enemy', and the general gaudy, showy nature of Viking warrior aristocracy, indeed all warrior aristocracy, it would be surprising if they did not have painted spear-shafts. As to continuance of Kragehul-style shaft decoration, this appears to have been not so much discontinued as transferred from the shaft to the socket of the spearhead. The use of the closed tubular socket, discussed above, which provided a clear unbroken surface probably led to this change. Surviving examples tended to use silver inlay to further ornament and enhance their elaborate interlace patterns.

The butt-spike, the spear's other head, was a Greek invention. As an important part of a hoplite's equipment, it was near-universal in the Greek phalanx, universal in the Roman army and, from the archaeological evidence, very common in the early Anglo-Saxon period. Yet they appear to be rare in Viking and pre-Viking Scandinavian warfare. Thus, despite the fact that the tactical picture, close-order infantry combat with spear and shield, remained unchanged, in the Anglo-Viking world the butt-spike barely registers in either archaeological or representational terms. It remained common in the Byzantine and Islamic worlds, yet we scrabble around to find rare examples such as the ninth-century Viking example from the Kilmainham-Islandbridge cemetery outside of Dublin. Now, it may be that given the butt-spike's small size compared to the spearhead, fewer have survived in the archaeological record. Equally, given the fact that they do not appear to have been as common in the pre-Viking and Early Anglo-Saxon world as they were in the Greco-Roman, it is possible that over time they fell more and more into disuse and had disappeared entirely by the end of the Anglo-Saxon Period. In tactical terms, this would mean that when the spearhead broke off then either the broken shaft continued to be used or else the broken spear was dropped and the sword was drawn.

Moving now onto missile weapons, we must now turn our attention to the bow (including the crossbow) and the javelin. The axe, as a missile, has already been discussed.

The *Maldon* poet tells us that in battle 'bows were busy' (*The Battle of Maldon* line 110), yet how effective was the archery of the period? Part of the reason for this lack of clarity derives from the fact that the true effectiveness of archery is, due to the number of variables at work, difficult to ascertain. The range is governed both by the calibre of the bow and by the strength of the archer, while as Coulston has correctly argued:

> the nature of the target, its size, vulnerability, rate of movement etc., also governs accuracy and effectiveness over various ranges.

The range of the Viking bow is unknown, although we are being a bit disingenuous calling it the 'Viking' bow. The finds from the princely boat grave at Hedeby,

Viking Warfare

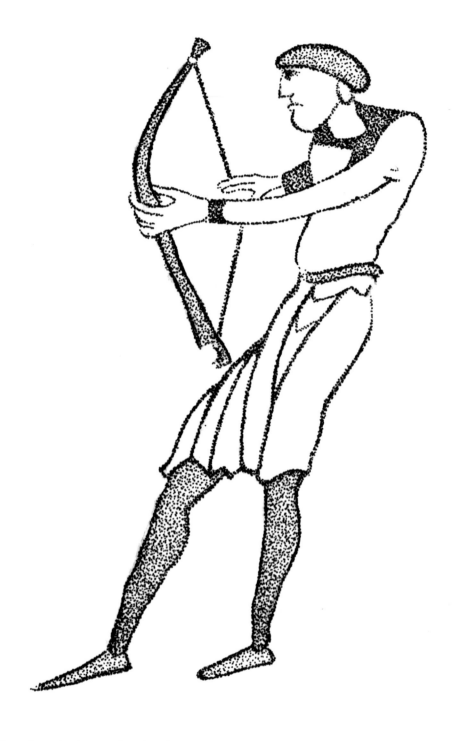

The solitary Anglo-Danish archer from the Bayeux Tapestry.

Chessell Down on the Isle of Wight, and Bifrons, as well as the bog deposits of Nydam, Thorsbjerg and Vimose, all show that the Vikings, the English and their ancestors employed the longbow. It is called the longbow to distinguish it from the crossbow – the short-bow is a myth, the Hedeby yew bow being 192 cm in length. However, even though the range of the weapon cannot be determined, its probable effectiveness can. Three pieces of evidence allow us to ascertain the probable effectiveness, if not the effective range, of the arrows of the period. These pieces of evidence are, firstly, the type of arrowheads used, secondly, the lid of the Franks Casket, and thirdly, descriptions of the weapon in *Beowulf* and *The Battle of Maldon*.

Arrowheads provide information on bowmanship in that they define both the perceived target areas and the probable penetrative power of the arrow. The absence of bodkin heads and the use of leaf-bladed heads by the Vikings points to their role in battle being an anti-personnel one, as opposed to an armour-piercing one. Equally, the Anglo-Saxons use of trilobate arrows was undoubtedly adopted by the Vikings. In the case of both leaf-bladed and trilobate heads, the edge takes predominance over the point; this is in order to maximise the level of damage when shooting at soft targets. Their primary function was thus to cause deep penetrating wounds and massive haemorrhaging. However, at extreme close range, and shooting with a flat trajectory, such arrowheads as were used by the Vikings may well have also been able to function in an armour-piercing role. The finds also convey status, for as well as the Hedeby ship burial, arrows have been found in the Ladeby, Gokstad and Oseberg ship graves, as well as in well-furnished warrior graves from Dublin, Orkney and Colonsay. Clearly the weapon was an acceptable part of a warrior's panoply.

This interpretation, of an anti-personnel as opposed to an armour-piercing role for archery, is supported by both the representational and literary evidence. The lid of the Franks Casket depicts what Wilson describes as 'a lost Old English legend concerning Egil'. The scene is of a man defending his hall with bow and arrow. The Casket is believed to be of Northumbrian manufacture and has been dated to the first half of the eighth century. The various items of military equipment depicted on the Franks Casket are believed to reflect accurately the equipment and fashions of the day. It is thus considered a credible source from which to determine the effectiveness of archery against both armoured and shielded warriors. The fifth figure from the left on the lid has most obviously succumbed to the archery and is unarmoured. Although no shield was depicted with this attacker, this does not pose a problem as the figure fourth from the left is depicted using a shield. This figure appears to be wearing body armour, probably a mail shirt, and is advancing, crouched behind his shield. The shield, although hit by two arrows, is depicted as being proof against this form of attack, as only the tips of the points of the arrows are shown to penetrate the shield, while most of the arrow projects outwards from the board. This image of the effectiveness of the shield against arrows, and thus the anti-personnel nature of early medieval archery, is further reinforced by the poetry.

The complete warrior 1 – an Anglo-Danish housecarl from the Bayeux Tapestry.

Beowulf (lines 3114–3119) states that warriors could be felled by arrows, but only by those arrows which passed over the shield wall, thus implying that the shield wall and thus the shield was an effective defence against arrows. While *The Battle of Maldon* (lines 265–72), describing the contribution made by the Northumbrian Æscferth, states that he shot many arrows, some of which found their mark: 'sometimes he ripped open a man'.

Before considering the effectiveness of the javelin, a mention must be made of the crossbow. The crossbow, like the mace, is a weapon that the Vikings potentially came into contact with both via their experiences in Scotland as well as on the Continent and at the Byzantine court. It is believed that crossbows are depicted on a number of Pictish stones, although this interpretation has recently been questioned. Comparisons can also be drawn between the weapons depicted on the Pictish stones and the late Roman/Byzantine *solenarion* or arrow-guide. Roman depictions of the crossbow are also not as unambiguous as Coulston believes, and as with the Pictish examples, the two third-century Gallo-Roman reliefs which purport to show crossbows more probably depict composite bows and arrow-guides. Whatsoever is the case, it impacts not at all on the current discussion, as in all cases the weapon is shown in a purely hunting context and there is no mention of the crossbow in a Viking or an Anglo-Danish military context prior to its use by the Normans during the invasion of AD 1066. Indeed, if we view the crossbow more as a weapon suited to siege warfare, then its use by the Normans and not by the Vikings becomes more understandable.

The arrowheads of the period were solely anti-personnel in nature; the same was also true of the javelins used during the same period. The Vikings preferred tanged, as opposed to socketed, angular and barbed styles. *The Battle of Maldon*, which of all the surviving poems emphasises the spear over the sword, describes the use of javelins solely in an anti-personnel capacity (*The Battle of Maldon* lines 134–158). At close range, the shield board could have been compromised by missiles; indeed, reconstructed Roman leaf-bladed javelins can, at a range of 10 m, penetrate 18 mm of oak and project their points 10 mm through the back of the wood.

THE WARRIOR

What constituted, in equipment terms, a warrior? The short answer is that it was a combination of the various artefacts described and discussed above. It did, however, go beyond this. It of course had cultural implications built around social status and duty. Viking culture was, like that of its counterparts the Franks and the Anglo-Saxons, one of gift and counter-gift. It was a world of heroic poetry and tales of great deeds. How ingrained such notions were in the psyche is of course debatable and, indeed, the question resembles discussion of the subject of chivalry. In both cases we are taking what is to some extent a literary construct and applying it to real-world situations. For if chivalry were seen as a set of rules

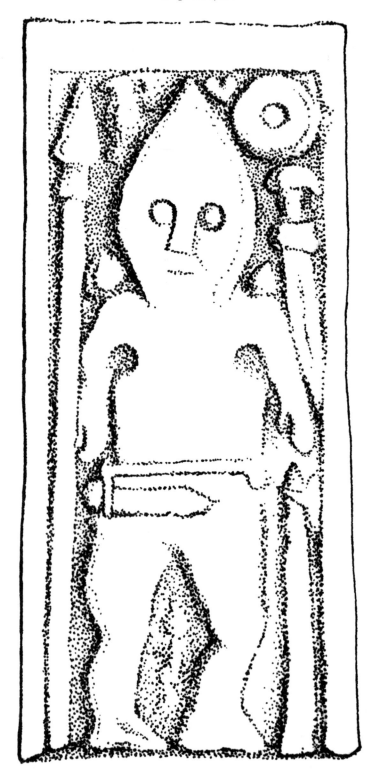

The complete warrior 2 – a Viking warrior surrounded by his weapons, from a Middleton cross fragment.

practised between individuals of a similar social standing, then it was, in this respect, similar to the world occupied by Viking warriors and their opponents. Both could be exceptionally cruel, heartless and ruthlessly realistic, yet good poetry and a heroic ideal cast a glamorous veneer over both.

Alongside this, we have an expectation of how the Vikings looked. As we have seen above there were no horned helmets; however, we still have a 'hairy barbarian' image, which in actuality could not be further from the truth. Body image and elite status go together. We have archaeological evidence stretching back to the Bronze Age in Northern Europe that male grooming was an important part of warrior culture. Toilet sets of nail and ear cleaners as well as tweezers are not unknown from male graves, while combs, clippers and razors are often found in male contexts. As well as making sure that hair and beard were well kept, the warrior would also have ensured that he was wearing the latest fashion. Writers about and practitioners of warfare from Ammianus to Napoleon have all understood the power of display. Improving your morale and lowering the enemy's came from, in part, looking good. The warriors who stormed ashore to sack monasteries and who stood in the shieldwall were, strange as it may sound, all acutely conscious of their appearance.

Thus, the complete warrior was a combination of a state of mind, a state of appearance and a set of military equipment. It is to that last point that we now turn.

When determining what constituted a complete set of military equipment, the best starting place is not burial evidence. Despite the fact that from an archaeological point of view graves are a valuable source of artefacts, very few of them contain viable weapons sets. Not, it should be noted, that this has ever stopped people using them for this purpose. The next place to turn, which is equally alluring and at least has the advantage of being closure to the reality of warfare than the burial rite, is the post-Viking legal codes. Codes such as the thirteenth-century Swedish *Upplandslagen* required infantrymen to have a shield, helmet, body armour, a spear and a sword, as well as a bow and thirty-six arrows. The Danes stipulated a sword, helmet, spear and shield. Meanwhile, in Norway the requirements were for axe, shield and spear, along with a bow and twenty-four arrows. What makes these later codes so attractive are the beliefs that they are not simply based upon earlier Viking Age laws, but that they actually contain fragments of older, possibly Viking, codes. Unfortunately, it is not possible to determine the date of these older elements. However, in their favour are the facts that the weapons sets described are not only viable, but also feasible in a Viking context and tally with contemporary legal requirements.

The two best sources for describing and articulating complete weapon sets are legal documents, but they are not exclusively Scandinavian in origin, although they are both Germanic in background. The first are the Frankish capitularies; the second, more detailed source, are the Anglo-Danish *heriots*. Kings, in an age of warrior aristocracy, needed to ensure that those who were weapon-worthy turned out for war properly equipped when summoned; not necessarily dripping in the latest state-of-the-art military hardware, but at least equipped to a minimum useable standard. In many ways, such laws reflect the realities of the social gradations within a warrior elite. Thus an individual may belong to this privileged group, but not necessarily be at the top and may indeed be simply in a position to provide no more than the basic requirement. Equally, as we shall see, these rules like the later Scandinavian laws we have mentioned above simply enumerate the bare requirements, the details of the provision being left to an individual.

In this we are also seeing a reflection of the reality that was practised so successfully by the Imperial Roman army. In the case of Rome an individual soldier was required to have a set of equipment in good working order, but there was not the uniformity that is so often assumed. Thus, body armour was, as far as the army was concerned, body armour and it did not matter if it was mail or scale; if an individual wanted a more highly decorated scabbard, well it was their money, as long as the sword still came out of it and was still able to do what swords do. The details revolve around function, not aesthetics. This is not to dismiss aesthetics, which were important; however, the capitularies and *heriots* existed to provide functioning military forces; aesthetics were there to show social differentiation within the group, secondary, certainly, but only marginally so.

Charlemagne at one point required his men to have shield, spear, long and short sword, a bow and a quiver of arrows. However, the Frankish and also slightly earlier Lombard laws did at times recognise the differences of social status within the group. Thus, to this list the *Capitulare Missorum* (AD 792–3) added, for those wealthy enough, horse and armour. Certainly the first list, with its inclusion of archery equipment, makes the belief that the later Scandinavian laws reflect the reality of the earlier Viking period understandable. Yet in a way, the archery equipment is the most problematical aspect; it does not appear in the Anglo-Danish stipulations we will discuss below, for by its very nature it was unheroic, but it must be explained. The roots of Viking warfare are Greek. It traces its ancestry to the clash of hoplites on the plains of Greece and they in their turn sprang out of the battles of the Mycenaean period. In this world of gods and heroes the tale which still stands tallest in our memory is that of Helen and the siege of Troy. Paris, the abductor of Helen, has great skill with a bow, as indeed does Odysseus, but, and it is a big but, even though his skill is described and complemented, it is viewed with not a little disdain. This view, the combination of necessity and distaste, continues up until the twentieth century. Kipling's poem *Arithmetic on the Frontier* replaces the bow with the marksman's rifle, but the meaning is the same. Such weapons are useful and they serve a valuable battlefield function – yet they are not heroic. True fame, true glory came from killing at close quarters, not at a distance.

For all that, pragmatism will out. Unheroic though it may be, the bow was too valuable a weapon to ignore. It can also be given a gloss of repectability. Thus, in *The Battle of the River Nissa* Harald Hardrada, the archetypal Viking, is praised for his skill with the bow, albeit in ship-to-ship combat. Meanwhile, in fifteenth-century England, noblemen, and even the king himself, were expected to be proficient with both longbow and crossbow. Heroics did not count when fighting for God and against Cathars, pagans and the infidel, for in AD 1200, the Church, despite earlier condemning the crossbow, now promoted the weapon in a 'just' cause.

The bow never really disappeared from the battlefield. It would be more surprising if it had. As a result, it appears in lists and codes of military equipment. Equally, when the circumstances were correct, such as ship-to-ship combat or when waiting for the tide to uncover a causeway, the bow would appear in the heroic poetry of the age. In these limited uses, particularly as a shipboard weapon, we see its currency in the Viking world and why it appears in later Scandinavian law codes. Its value on the battlefields of the day and low ranking in the list of required military equipment stems in part from its unheroic nature, but equally from the fact that it was never deployed in large enough numbers to make a decisive impression. This latter point springs from the circular argument that the bow did not win battles because it was never deployed in large enough numbers, and so we go round. The Romans, and later the Normans at Hastings, fielded large numbers of archers; however, the success of both groups came from combined-arms forces, not from any intrinsic superiority possessed by bowmen *per se*.

Heriots provide a window on the military equipment of the complete warrior in an Anglo-Danish/late Anglo-Saxon context. They also conveniently open a window on the levels of equipment that the different ranks within the weapons-bearing elite were expected to have. *Heriots* (from *here-geatu* or war-gear) were a form of death-duty. All those of thegnly rank or above were required to arrange for the payment of a set quantity of military equipment to their lord on their death. Although the payment could be remitted to cash, and usually was in the Danelaw, in general military equipment was paid, with the level or amount being determined by rank.

Thus, in II Cnut 71 an earl's *heriot* consisted of 8 horses (4 saddled, 4 unsaddled), 4 helmets, 4 byrines (mail shirts), 4 swords, 8 spears, 8 shields and 200 *mancuses* of gold; a king's thegn was expected to pay 4 horses (2 saddled, 2 unsaddled), 1 helmet, 1 byrine, 2 swords, 4 spears, 4 shields and 50 *mancuses* of gold; while a lesser thegn paid 1 saddled horse plus one each of helmet, byrine, sword, spear and shield, as well as a lesser amount of money. In the Danelaw, according to II Cnut 71, the *heriots* of a king's thegn with soke and of a lesser thegn were simple money payments (£4 & £2 respectively); only a king's thegn closer to the king was expected to supply arms as well, specifically 2 horses (1 saddled, 1 unsaddled), 1 sword, 2 spears, 2 shields and 50 *mancuses* of gold.

How then do we interpret II Cnut 71, which is, it must be remembered, corroborated in level of payment terms by surviving contemporaneous Anglo-Saxon wills?

Heriots, as set amounts of money or military equipment (arms, armour and horses) plus money dependant upon rank, may have simply been related to rank and the deceased's ability to pay, and as with earlier grave goods, have been, or should be seen as, simply symbolic of rank and status. They should thus (following this explanation) not be equated to the actual military equipment carried by the various ranks or levels of society into battle. This explanation, although possible, is not terribly plausible. The usual view that *heriots* represented the battlefield equipment of the various levels of society engaged in warfare remains the most likely interpretation; however, the question remains – what is the key?

Brooks believes that the 'most probable' reconstruction for the earl's *heriot* is 'for four fully armed soldiers (each with helmet, byrine, sword, spear, shield and saddled horse) and four attendants armed only with spear and shield.' The problem with Brooks' interpretation is the four attendants, whom he muses may have been grooms and may have ridden, bareback, the unsaddled horses; equally, the unsaddled horses may have been reliefs or pack-horses.

The attendants take us to the heart of the problem – namely, what constituted a viable weapon set? Was a spear and shield enough? Were the attendants, if they existed and if they were so armed, viable? The answer to these latter two questions is of course no. While we know that Anglo-Saxon armies had a logistic train (see Bede, *Historia Ecclesiastica*, IV.22 and the story of Imma), there was no need for it to be armed, because that was not its job, and there was certainly no need for it to be badly armed. Anyone armed simply with spear and shield was not only unviable, they were a positive liability. Why? Because they lacked either an axe or a sword. The Maldon poet rightly stresses the importance of the spear in the warfare of the period, but at some point the fighting would come down to the edge of the sword. Anyone not equipped for this stage of battle with sword or axe was a liability both physically and in terms of morale.

Thus, the minimum viable weapons set was a shield, and a spear, and a sword. Even in that closest of close-order formations, the Macedonian pike phalanx, every man carried a sword. The Vikings, the Anglo-Saxons and, in the context of *heriots*, the Anglo-Danish monarchy fielded properly equipped forces. We are dealing here with the wars of aristocratic warrior elites and their armed followers, and as a result *heriots* were used to provide viable sets of military equipment. Thus, the answer to the question – what was the key? The sword was the key; the number of swords equals the number of viable weapons sets and thus the number of men a *heriot* was designed to equip. Loyn, in his *The Governance of Anglo-Saxon England 500–1087*, when speaking of *heriots*, states:

> The basic impression, however, is clear and sound. Earls and thegns were men magnificently equipped for the warfare of the age.

That is what we see when we look at II Cnut 71 and surviving late Anglo-Saxon wills. Yes, attendants would have been present, but as unarmed servants; they would not have been equipped in such a way as to make them incapable of combat and thus liable to run away at the first hint of trouble. Thus, in II Cnut 71 an earl's *heriot* equipped four armoured men, while that of a king's thegn equipped one body-armoured, and one un-body-armoured man. As for the extra shields and spears, in all of the cases where they occur, we also have unsaddled horses. These horses would have probably doubled as both relief and pack-horses, and in the latter capacity they would have carried those things which all the evidence shows to have been somewhat fragile, definitely disposable, yet vital, namely (spare) shields and spears.

The Frankish, English and later Scandinavian sources are all telling us the same thing. On top of this, the evidence they contain fits well within our understanding of the warfare of the period. We are thus left with a coherent picture which allows us not simply to articulate the minimum level but to also paint in gradations. A viable weapon set was a shield, spear and sword or axe. You need something to kill with once the spear point has been passed and a knife or short *seax* is too small. Indeed, in the latter case we are looking more at a hunting tool. Above this basic level of shield, spear and sword we see the addition of armour and, potentially, the carrying of an increasing number of weapons. The basic pieces of armour were the shield and the helmet. The shield protects the body while the helmet covers the head. Body armour and extra armour such as greaves are useful but not a necessity. Where little armour is worn, its value is basically individual; it is only when we start to see armoured ranks that we begin to gain a cumulative effect, a sort of herd immunity similar to vaccination. What we see, particularly with the wearing of body armour, is an expression of social standing; the same is true to some extent with the carrying of extra weapons, for alongside sword and spear can be added javelins, bow and *seax*, again useful but not necessary. The constraints of close-order infantry combat are, in equipment terms, not terrible rigorous: the spear to create the gap and the tear; the sword to widen, exploit and rout; and, overall, the shield to protect you while you are doing it.

5

'Hold Their Shields Aright'

Line 20 of the poem *The Battle of Maldon* sees Byrhtnoth extolling his men to, as the chapter title tells us, 'hold their shields aright' in the face of the Viking threat. It is not recorded, but something very similar was undoubtedly being said on the Viking side. Why was this so and why was the Viking and Anglo-Saxon way of war the same? What, for that matter, was their way of war? Where then does Viking warfare fit? Did the Vikings and their opponents engage in different types of warfare? The short answer is that Viking warfare belongs within Western warfare. The Vikings did engage in different types of warfare, but it was the warfare of pitched battles between close-order infantry, and of mounted and seaborne raids. It was thus non-ritual; they did not indulge in ritual warfare or war as play.

The Viking was a close-order infantryman. But what did that mean in practice? What types of formation were used and what exactly were the roles of cavalry and archers in Viking warfare?

In order to answer these questions we must turn to the Vikings' enemies. Earlier Anglo-Saxon literary sources such as Bede and Eddius Stephanus, although they may record the fact that battles occurred, provide no information on the deployment of troops and merely confine themselves to recording who won and who lost. The later sources, however, do at least name and to some extent describe tactical formations and it is from these that any understanding of the battlefield formations of the period must start.

The heroic poems *Beowulf* (lines 3117–8), *The Battle of Maldon* (lines 102, 242 and 277), and *The Battle of Brunanburh* (line 5) all describe armies as being drawn up for battle in a formation known as a 'shield wall'. The shield wall is also mentioned in Asser's *Life of King Alfred* (37) and, of course, in the Anglo-Saxon Chronicle entry for 937. In none of these cases is the shield wall actually described in detail, nor indeed should these sources be expected to provide such a description, as they are neither military manuals nor, for that matter, are they written for an audience ignorant of the subject matter.

What then was a shield wall? Modern interpretations tend to see it as a line of men whose overlapping or interlocking shields created a solid barrier or *wall* of shields. Is this interpretation correct? The simple answer is no. Firstly, this interpretation is guilty of taking a poetic term far too literally, and creating a wall of shields. Part of the reason for this, and one of the reasons why this interpretation has gained common currency, derives from the fact that writers in the Anglo-Saxon period, wishing to display their erudition, incorrectly used the Latin word *testudo* (they failed to grasp the precise military meaning of the word) for the old English term *bordweall*. The problem of the interlocking shields interpretation has been further exacerbated by two very well known sources connected with the Battle of Hastings – namely the Bayeux Tapestry and William of Poitiers.

The Bayeux Tapestry does indeed show a shield wall of overlapping shields. However, the scene is implausible, for the troops are so closely packed together that their weapons, particularly their double-handed battle-axes, are rendered unusable. Rather, the scene on the Tapestry should be read as simply representing a large number of troops in close-order. Equally, William of Poitiers' statement that the English 'were so densely massed that the dead could scarcely fall' should be read in the same light. If taken literally, it becomes as ludicrous as a literal belief that the French dead at Agincourt lay piled 'higher than a man'. The final part of the problem lies in the fact that in the Germanic world the shield was a very high status object and thus it is unsurprising that the word, the object, was used to describe an important formation.

Again the question – what, then, was the shield wall? The answer is really quite simple, and was hit upon quite some time ago, but subsequently largely ignored:

> [it] is of course merely a poetical expression for a wall-like line of shielded men. It has nothing to do with interlocking shields.
>
> > Sir Charles Oman 1924, *A History of The Art of War in the Middle Ages Volume One: 378–1278 AD*, p.71 fn.1.

In this definition Oman is, however, merely echoing Vegetius (*Epitoma Rei Militaris*, II.17), who stated that in battle the heavy infantry

> stood *so to speak like a wall of iron* [my italics], fighting it out.

The formation was a fighting formation – it merely looked like a wall, as indeed is shown both on Trajan's Column (scene LXX) and in the fifth-century Vatican Vergil (folio 66v). Equally it could be described as a 'spear wall' and certainly if this term were used, then our understanding would be different.

Thus Viking warriors, like their earlier counterparts, stood, as Vegetius tells us, wall-like, but they fought and killed primarily, as Herodian (IV.10.3) points out, with a spear. *Wall* was merely a poetic way of describing a close-order formation. Indeed, the shield wall was no more static or immobile than a hoplite, or a Macedonian phalanx, for the men in a shield wall, phalanx, or *foulkon* were expected to advance, in formation, and kill the enemy. The killing, as will be seen, was done using 'fire and shock'.

Before, however, going on to consider the 'face of shield wall battle', we must first turn to that other formation used by English and Viking forces in the period under study, namely the wedge. The most detailed description of the formation is found in *The History of the Danes* by Saxo Grammaticus. Unfortunately, not only is the work thirteenth-century in date, but Saxo's history is more noted for the style of his language than for the quality of his research, which is poor at best. As for the Poetic Edda and the Sagas, as sources they are of little use, for besides date and quality problems, they simply provide the title of the formation without providing a description. Turning to the Roman sources, Ammianus' (XVII.13.9) *caput porci* was *angustum fronte* or narrow-fronted, and that is about the limit of his description. Vegetius is more loquacious on the subject of the wedge; in book 3 chapter 9 of his *Epitome Rei Militaris* he describes a formation 'narrower in front and broad behind', which was designed to break an enemy's line by concentrating a large number of missiles onto a portion of the opposing shield wall.

What then was a wedge? There are basically two schools of thought. The first school simply and uncritically follows Saxo's description of successive ranks of either 2, 4, 8, etc. or 2, 3, 4, 5, etc. men to produce a very pointy wedge. The second, promoted by Delbrück, argues that the wedge was in fact a column of attack. Certainly, if one looks at a pig or boar's head and snout the pointy model does not fit the name, nor does it entirely match a column of attack, although the latter does provide a closer fit.

There is no easy solution to the problem of what a wedge actually looked like, for with all questions of this nature it comes down to a reading, an interpretation of the admittedly limited evidence.

Saxo's description, although detailed, provides for an over-complex, probably unworkable formation. It is also true that his description does not fit with the more reliable picture painted by Vegetius. The view of the wedge in the *Epitome Rei Militaris* accords more with a column of attack. What is more, the column of attack is easy to form and manoeuvre, is fast (certainly compared to advancing in line) and can break through a line; it thus fits all of the wedge's criteria. The use of columns of attack also accords with one of the rare tactical descriptions present in Anglo-Saxon literature. Asser's *Life of King Alfred* (37–9) describes how an English army attacked uphill, in two divisions, and defeated their Viking opponents. Although the English were initially drawn up in a shield wall, Asser (*Life of King Alfred* 38) goes on to state that, 'when he [Alfred] had closed up the shield wall in proper order, he moved his army without delay against the enemy'. The closing up of the shieldwall implies a change of formation; this impression is further reinforced by the fact that the English moved forward 'without delay'. Advancing in line is a slow, tricky business, as the line must be constantly dressed in order to ensure that it remains straight. The evidence (Asser) thus suggests that Alfred reorganised his line into columns of attack, which are far easier to manoeuvre, keep their formation without the need for constant dressing, and can move (even uphill) relatively quickly. Given the fact that Alfred's attack was uphill and in the face of the enemy's missiles, the benefits of a column are obvious.

The phrase 'pig's head', as our Roman sources are at pains to point out, was no more than soldier's slang. We may thus be placing too much credence on an inexact description of a formation. With this in mind, it is worth noting that the same is also true of Agathias' description of the Franks at the Battle of the Casilinus River in 554. Agathias (2.8) tells us that the Franks' wedge formation 'was *like* a triangular figure *resembling* the letter delta' (my italics). Haldon, in his *The Byzantine Wars*, views the wedge simply as two columns of attack which 'converged at the head', forming a hollow trapezoidal formation, and in this interpretation we are probably getting close to the truth of the wedge.

Leaving aside Saxo and soldier's slang the wedge, as a formation, makes most sense as a column of attack – a formation known for its ability to advance quickly, to be hard to completely disrupt, and to have the potential to break lines. However, it is probable that the formation was not parade-ground neat. Thus, while the front ranks (the snout?) comprising the war-leader and his housecarls maintained formation, it is equally possible that the back end of the column was not so neat and spread slightly, forming a trapezoidal or pig's head-shaped column.

Returning to the shield wall, the next questions we must attempt to answer with respect to the shield wall are concerned with depth and organisation. Depth has no certain answer; even turning to our Roman sources, we gain no definite solution for the depth to which the Imperial Roman Army deployed. Josephus and Vegetius describe (and, in the case of the latter, favour) a three/six deployment, whereas Arrian and Maurice prefer a four/eight solution. Thus Roman infantry, and it is very likely that the Vikings, and their opponents for that matter, followed the same pattern, normally deployed in lines three or four ranks deep, employing deeper six- or eight-rank formations when facing cavalry. There was undoubtedly, in both the Roman and Viking worlds, no hard and fast rule concerning line depth, and the use of 3/6 and 4/8 in warfare was probably very dependant upon circumstances and the numbers involved. Although it is very unlikely that they deployed in ranks less than three deep, as such a two or one rank deep formation would lack solidity, would be easily breached by cavalry or infantry, and would swiftly collapse, leading to ruin and rout.

To the Greeks, the right of the line was the place of honour. From what we can deduce of Anglo-Saxon and Anglo-Danish organisation, it appears that the centre of the line had precedence and, as we have nothing to say otherwise, the same was also probably true of the Vikings as well. However, it must be admitted that the evidence for this is slight, as it is merely implied in the *Battle of Maldon* (lines 17-24) and only explicitly stated of Harold II at Hastings, in the *Carmen de Hastingae Proelio*.

At Hastings, Harold stood among his housecarls. The housecarls, a creation of Cnut, have at times been seen as something new. Yet in truth, Cnut's creation did not come out of a clear blue sky. Rather, it was based upon the household troops (*comitatus*) of the English and Danish courts and aristocracy. The housecarls were thus probably no more than an expansion in terms of numbers and a formalisation in terms of structure of an existing and well-known institution. In terms of numbers and primary function, the housecarls, from Cnut to Harold II, provided the king with a large body of full-time professional warriors. It was certainly not large enough to allow the king to fight a war without calling upon the forces of the *fyrd*, but it was of a size to provide a formidable core to any royal army. We also know from Siward's 1054 campaign in Scotland (Anglo-Saxon Chronicle D manuscript) that the great nobles in the realm also maintained their own forces of housecarls. This of course should come as no surprise, for the housecarls were no different to Byrhtnoth's hearth-troop (*The Battle of Maldon*, line 24), or for that matter to Hnaef's:

> nor ever did a man's own brave companions make better payment for the white mead than his young warriors made to Hnaef.

The Fight at Finnsburg, lines 37–40

As for the organisation of the rest of the shield wall, while we can, in institutional terms, understand the basic tactical unit, we can only surmise with regard to the order of battle. Thus while the *fyrd*, be it a full royal host or an earl's army, was organised as Abels argues, along divisions based upon shires, hundreds and private sokes, the basic tactical building blocks were the contingents of the nobles, with those who owed service direct to the king being marshalled and commanded by their local sheriff. Thus in the late, as in the early, Anglo-Saxon period, lords and their armed retainers played the main role in warfare and in the make-up of English armies. The same was true for Viking forces. Here, though, particularly when looking at what the Anglo-Saxon Chronicle calls raiding armies, we should look at the ship's crew (*skibara*) as the basic tactical unit and build formations up from there. Indeed, just as the Anglo-Saxon word *fyrd* has as its root meaning 'to journey', so too the Scandinavian word *lith*, which also meant originally to journey, particularly by sea, came to mean a fleet and thus, like *fyrd*, an armed force. Again, a *lith* as a force is a rather amorphous term and cannot be said to equate to a set number. Thus it could be a single ship, or the leader of the *lith* could attract followers who themselves owned and commanded ships. It is in this latter case that we should view the Great Raiding Armies which ravaged England. Leadership was most definitely heroic and charismatic in nature. Success and generosity had a major impact on the size of the force that could be fielded.

How these units were arranged when, to rephrase *The Battle of Maldon* line 22, the troops were suitably arrayed, can only be a matter of conjecture. There was undoubtedly a known order of precedence based upon social rank used to array units, possibly similar to the status system which the Greeks used to place contingents from different city states in the same line of battle and ensure that they were correctly ordered. It is possible that the higher the rank of a unit's commander, the closer to the centre of the line it was placed.

Now, we should not delude ourselves into thinking that these formations that we have just described, wall and wedge, were late creations, the product of contact with more *sophisticated* continental neighbours. Rather, the panoply of a large shield, thrusting spear and slashing sword was a constant of Viking warfare and consequently so were the tactical formations that went with it. Viking warfare, and for that matter its Vendel-period predecessor, was a part of the mainstream, in terms of equipment, techniques and tactics, of the Western way of war, and that should not be forgotten.

Before we turn to the mechanics of combat, let us briefly (the evidence lets us do no other) consider the question of training. War for the Vikings, Franks and Anglo-Saxons was, as articulated in the case of the latter by Abels, but with equal relevance to all, the preserve of the nobility and their armed retainers. Even these retainers, however, had social standing. To be weapons-worthy you had to come from the correct social background. Society was structured and hierarchical, with those at and close to the very top forming the ruling warrior elite. Hunting was and remains an aristocratic pastime not because it was an amusing entertainment (which it has subsequently evolved into) but because it was, and for a very long time, good preparation for the rigours of combat. For hunting taught not just the obvious weapons skills but also improved an individual's riding, stamina (one could be in the field all day), team work and reliance on others, and the ability to take and give orders, not to mention violence, aggression and the ability to kill.

Aside from hunting as a trainer of warriors, we also see, in the Anglo-Saxon world at least, bands of youths living, exercising and training together, all of which we see in Bede's *Life of St Cuthbert*. St Wilfrid also seems to have been on the verge of a similar upbringing but chose the Church instead. As the 'children' in such bands got older, so their deeds spread beyond simple exercise to attacking neighbouring territory and it is this stage of a young nobleman's development that is most likely being described in the poem *Wulf and Eadwacer*. Such bands would have been under the protection of a local lord and we see this in *De Gestis Herwardi Saxonis*, the life of Hereward the Wake, who joins such a band of youth at the house of his godfather. Adoption, both formal or semi-formal, going to live with a god- or step-father who was socially superior and/or had a reputation as a great warrior, was another method of gaining martial experience.

Of course, the best way to learn was of course to do. However, before we turn to that, we have a passage from the Carolingian world to consider, specifically from Nithard's *Histories*, III.6. According to Nithard the following practice exercise was quite common, although whether he means generally or simply within the Carolingian Empire is another matter. Simply, two teams, both on horseback, would take it in turns to charge their opponents, then turn away and be pursed before turning again to become the pursuer. This produced, due to the excellence of the execution of these manoeuvres, good disciple.

Finally, of course, the best place to learn warfare was the battlefield itself, with training going through a number of stages. However, we need not view it in quite such formal terms; rather, it was just a part of development, of 'growing-up'.

It possibly simply started with watching, but most likely the first introduction to the 'place of slaughter' may well have been skirmishing with javelins against similar youths. From there, shield wall combat was learned from the rear ranks, with age, experience and (undoubtedly) social status propelling an individual through the ranks to the front. Training was a product of experience. Julius Caesar (*Gallic War* VI.21) viewed Germanic life as one of warfare and hunting and this, for the young Viking, was still as true in the ninth century AD as in the first century BC; each built on the other, and the more you did of both, the more chance you had (theoretically) of surviving. The Imperial Roman Army had a very set training regime, but this did not exist in the world that followed; there was no Renaissance, no New Model in the early medieval period. Instead, doing, watching, fostering, hunting, talking, stories, games, sparring were all a part of the education and lifestyle of the Vikings and their contemporaries and it was as a result of all of these that a warrior was trained and stayed trained.

We must now turn to the questions of combat, symmetry, and how these formations worked in practice.

At Marathon in 490 BC, the opposing battle-lines were drawn up approximately 1.5 km apart and it is believed that the Greeks ran the last 200–300 metres. Was the extreme distance covered at a run at Marathon the killing zone of the Persian archers? Probably. If so, then the same conditions did not apply in Viking Age England for, as will be seen below, archery, although it played a part in Anglo-Viking warfare, was never of any great significance. In Viking warfare the killing zone had a depth of some thirty yards, the maximum effective range of the javelin. Our sources do not tell us how this distance was crossed. The problems for close-order infantry in crossing a killing zone concern speed and cohesion. For the faster a line or shield wall moves, the more likely it is to cease being a line, to loose cohesion and be easier to break and destroy, as it would, on reaching the enemy, already possess natural gaps and tears which could be exploited. Equally, if we add into the equation the weight of the equipment (and it must be remembered that the shield must be held out from the body in order to function correctly), crossing too great a distance at a run would tire a warrior and reduce combat effectiveness. It is, however, probable that, given 30 yards is only about as many paces, this distance was crossed in less than a minute at a quick walking pace. Where the depth of the killing zone was greater, such as at the Battle of Ashdown in 871, where Alfred was forced to attack uphill (see Asser's *Life of King Alfred*, 37–39), a shield wall or line would not serve; thus we see the English forming columns in order to cross the distance with alacrity without sacrificing cohesion in the process.

Shield walls worked in general terms by using 'fire and shock'; even if, as at Maldon, the 'fire' (bows and javelins) was not that effective, it was still employed in an attempt to overcome the problem of symmetry. In *Judith*, the missile attack (in this case spears) was accompanied by a huge roar, which was possibly the Anglo-Saxon version of what the Romans termed the *barritus*. Our sources make clear (see particularly Asser) that loud shouting was a feature of the warfare of the period and not confined to the English. As for the reintroduction of a missile capability (the javelin) into the hoplite panoply, that was Roman in origin. The symmetry, in military terms, stemmed from the fact that in battle the arms, equipment, tactics and training were the same for the Vikings and their English opponents. Victory, therefore, was dependant upon other factors: morale, luck (such as the death of Byrhtnoth at Maldon), numbers, even possibly the weight of missiles failing on a shield wall prior to contact. The Battle of Hastings in 1066 was lost, or won, depending upon your perspective, because the sides were asymmetrical; even so, it was still not an easy victory.

The Maldon poet's emphasis of, and concentration on, the spear is perfectly correct and normal, for in the shield wall, when the lines met, and in the pursuit, it was the main weapon of death. For when the lines met, the killing took place at a distance of less than the length of a spear. At this stage of the fighting the spear was thrust or thrown, depending upon what target opportunity was presented. However, unlike in the Roman or early Anglo-Saxon periods, the butt-spike appears to have been little used, even though the tactical situation which had created it remained. Rather once the spear was lost or its head was broken, the warrior reverted to sword or axe in order to beat down his opponent, and to break the enemy's line. As to the actual mechanics of this form of combat, little can be said. They fought, they killed, and they hacked (or at least tried to) their way into the enemy's shield wall with sword or axe. For a heroic warrior aristocracy this was the epitome of their existence, what they had lived for, been bred for, and been trained to do since childhood – everything came together on the field of battle. Indeed, this is articulated in the Anglo-Saxon poem *Judith*:

> Swiftly then with their gleaming swords those valiant heroes made an inroad through the thick of their foes; they hacked at shields and sheared through the shield wall.

Mounted combat. A detail from the tenth-century Gosforth Cross. (Redrawn by M. Daniels from Bailey 1980)

Once the lines had met, and particularly in this age of heroic leadership, when commanders fought in the front rank of the shield wall, control of the battle very much ceased and events were left to take their course. Harold II at Hastings appears to have been unusual in that he may not have stood in the very front of the battle, and thus was able to issue orders and attempt to control events. Equally, Hastings was unusual in that it lasted all day, and in that the enemy attacked in waves, with retreats and lulls in between bouts of activity. Normally, when battle was joined the conflict was short and swift, with no respite in the fighting until one side gave way. For the object, once the shield walls met, was to defeat the enemy. Victory was achieved either by the infliction of some catastrophic event such as the death of a leader (the death of Byrhtnoth at Maldon being the obvious example), or by the swift breaking of the enemy's shield wall, and this, we may imagine, is what Alfred achieved at Ashdown and Athelstan at Brunanburh, particularly as in the latter case the pursuit lasted all day, thereby implying a swift victory.

The breaking of the shield wall was important because if one side could punch a hole through the other's line then their opponents' unshielded backs would become vulnerable, their morale would in all probability collapse, and thus the enemy's line could be easily rolled up. The whole bloody process of creating tears and gaps by killing the enemy at close quarters and by fighting your way into and through your opponents' line was all with the sole purpose of causing the disruption, loss of cohesion and disintegration of the shield wall that you were trying to defeat. This was how battles were won. Each side was, of course, trying to achieve the same ends with the same basic material – thus symmetry. Technological or equipment solutions to the problem of symmetry were, of course, rapidly adopted by all sides; in this period such a solution was the broad or Danish axe, which first appeared around the millennium and which may well have been developed and adopted partly in order to break shield walls. Its other martial use was concerned with the rise of cavalry. However, a third use was purely concerned with status and display, for a number of figures on the Bayeux Tapestry, in courtly as opposed to battlefield settings, appear unarmoured, yet holding a broad axe as a mark of martial prowess.

Of course, the alternative to the swift collapse and the catastrophic event was slow attrition, and again an obvious example presents itself. The slow haemorrhaging of the Anglo-Danish monarchy's army at Hastings in 1066 meant that at the end of the day their shield wall lacked the ability, the stability, to withstand the final Norman assault.

The collapse, once it occurred, would have been swift and then the pursuit would have begun. Casualty figures are impossible to ascertain; the best that can be said is that in this type of warfare the loosing side usually suffers far higher casualties than the victors, and that the majority of a defeated side's casualties will have occurred at this stage. This is why our sources refer to such events as slaughter, for indeed a pursuit could and frequently did produce a charnel house. For a victorious Viking army the initial phase of the pursuit would have been on foot, but the horses would have been swiftly brought up and then the mounted phase would have begun, and this phase would have lasted until night or terrain intervened. Whether on foot or horse, the spear was the ideal weapon of pursuit, as it had the edge over the sword in terms of length of reach.

> There in the dust fell the main part of the muster-roll of the Assyrian nobility, of that odious race. Few survivors reached their native land.
>
> *Judith*

CAVALRY

> An earl belongs on a charger's back; a mounted troop must ride in regular array, and the foot-soldier stand firm.
>
> *Maxims I*

As we can see from the quote from *Maxims I* above, the horse was used by the Anglo-Saxons for military transport; strategic mobility, in other words. We also know that the Vikings used it for exactly the same purpose. This is hardly surprising, as the horse was used for this purpose well into the twentieth century. But what of the horse's other military application – that of a fighting platform? Did the Vikings use it for this purpose? Did the Vikings have cavalry? Certainly, their descendants the Normans had no problems at becoming adept at the art of mounted combat – indeed, they are still famous for it today.

Archaeologically, there have been a number of finds of horse gear in graves from the Scandinavian Vendel period, some of which also included weaponry. These finds, however, neither prove nor disprove mounted combat. As to the types of weapons found in the horse burials, they are high-status weapons (sword, seax and axe), although spears and shield fittings were also deposited. In terms of usage, although none of the weapons were specifically designed for mounted combat, it is also true to say that none of the weapons could not have been used on horseback for, with the single exception of the bow, all of the weapons used by the Vikings could have been used with equal efficiency on both foot and horseback. As for the period under study, we have, from this country, a number of finds of stirrups, spurs, bits, as well as a part of a Viking-period saddle from York. Equally, the ubiquitous manuscript illustrations of puttees point to a horsey, riding society. Puttees, contrary to popular belief, were not worn to keep the lower leg warm; rather, they were an important piece of riding equipment.

Representational evidence for mounted combat, and here we must spread the net wide to hopefully provide a context for the Viking period, is provided by the depictions of mounted Anglo-Saxon warriors on the reverse of the cross-slab at Aberlemno, Angus (Aberlemno no. 2), and on Die Design 2, 'Rider and Fallen Warrior', from the Sutton Hoo helmet. In the case of the Aberlemno example,

Northumbrians are shown on horseback engaged in combat with both foot and mounted opponents, while the Sutton Hoo example depicts a warrior riding down his opponent. Both depictions show the mounted warriors protected by shields and fighting with spears or javelins, all of which is perfectly feasible and probably represented the reality of the mounted combat of the day. The use of the javelin from horseback is an accepted method of combat and is attested from both earlier Roman sources, such as Arrian's second-century work on tactics (*Ars Tactica*, 42), and later sources such as the eleventh-century Bayeux Tapestry. Depictions of mounted combat with weapons other than the spear are unfortunately lacking, although the Repton Stone does show a single figure of a mounted warrior brandishing sword(?) and shield. The fact that the Sutton Hoo example can be closely paralleled by symbolic depictions of cavalrymen on both Greek and Roman tombstones does not affect the validity of the scene; the riding down of a foot soldier is an accepted method of mounted combat. However, in the case of Die Design 2, 'Rider and Fallen Warrior', from the Sutton Hoo helmet, a caveat must be added. The Swedish antecedents of the helmet from mound 1 at Sutton Hoo may possibly mean that the scene depicts the realities of Swedish as opposed to Anglo-Saxon warfare, particularly in the light of Engström's argument that mounted warfare was a common part of Swedish (Vendel) warfare in this period. If this argument is correct, then the ancestors of the Vikings and, presumably, the Vikings themselves were no strangers to mounted combat. As well as the Swedish evidence, we also have the cultural interaction between the Jutland peninsula and the Carolingian Empire and the Carolingians definitely engaged in mounted combat.

The Viking-period (dated to between AD 930 and 1020) Neston cross Fragment 5 Face C, although it has been compared to the reverse of the cross-slab at Aberlemno, Angus (Aberlemno no. 2), does not aid our understanding of mounted combat in the early Anglo-Saxon period due to the lateness of its date. Its depiction of a 'joust' is unusually early; however, leaving that aside, its value in terms of the use of horses/mounted forces in combat is in the main confined to the fact that it provides, as White argues, 'further confirmation that mounted horsemen used spears.'

As for the Bayeux Tapestry, the work merely serves to confirm and contextualise Harold Godwinson, and by extension the Anglo-Danish warrior elite, as a part of the European mainstream not only in terms of equipment, but also in that militarily he was perfectly at home on horse or foot.

The literary evidence, along with a number of manuscript illustrations, points to the use of the horse as a means of transport to battle; it also supports the thesis that the Anglo-Saxons and, by extension, the Vikings were capable of engaging in mounted combat. The primary example of the former is *The Battle of Maldon* (lines 2–3), although Eddius Stephanus' *Life of Wilfrid* (19) provides the earliest piece of evidence for a mounted force when it describes King Ecgfrith as commanding a mounted host. Examples of the latter are provided by the Anglo-Saxon Chronicle entries for 937 and 1016.

All day long the West Saxons with elite cavalry pressed in the tracks of the hateful
nation, with mill-sharp blades severely hacked from behind those who fled battle.

Anglo-Saxon Chronicle, A manuscript, 937

The Battle of Brunanburh, as the quote above shows, was more a pursuit than
a battle; Athelstan and his host rapidly overthrew the enemy shield wall, and
the English then mounted, bloodily pursuing the vanquished enemy for as long
as the daylight lasted. We are less well informed about other English mounted
pursuits. In 1016 (according to the F manuscript of the Anglo-Saxon Chronicle),
King Edmund, at some point prior to his defeat at Ashingdon, pursued Cnut's
raiders. Both sides appear to have been mounted and although we cannot for
certain ascertain the reason for the breaking off of the chase, it does appear that
Edmund's forces were able to cut up the enemy's rearguard. The use, and value,
of mounted forces in a pursuit capacity was well known to the Vikings and they
used it where possible. The fact that at times, as in AD 937, they were on the
receiving end should be seen simply as a result of the vagaries of warfare and not
as a lack of ability.

Harold Godwinson presents us with a potentially well-documented series of
examples of the value of mounted forces to a warleader brought up partly in
the Viking tradition. According to the D manuscript entry of the Anglo-Saxon
Chronicle for 1063, Earl Harold led a force to Rhuddlan and, although he
surprised Gruffydd and burnt his hall, his quarry escaped, albeit temporarily.
Florence of Worcester, expanding (yet again) upon the Anglo-Saxon Chronicle,
states that the English force consisted of a 'small troop of horsemen'. Harold's
Welsh strategy, of rapid movement and surprise, was of course repeated a few years
later when as king he marched north to York and his greatest battlefield success. It
is also reminiscent of what we can glean of Ecgfrith's plan for the Nechtanesmere
campaign. In the latter case, Ecgfrith (according to Eddius Stephanus in his *Life
of Bishop Wilfrid* [19]) led a mounted host, and thus it is likely that Florence is
correct and that Harold's force was also mounted. This is hardly surprising for
two reasons. Firstly, a small, fast (and therefore mounted) force was the best
means of achieving Harold's end, namely that of taking the enemy at unawares
in the middle of his own territory, and secondly, and to some extent obviously,
all of the evidence points to the fact that English warriors rode to battle. Having
said all of that, however, Harold's Welsh raid, and for that matter his rapid
marches north and then south in 1066, merely show him taking full advantage
of the mounted, and thus potentially highly mobile, nature of Anglo-Danish
armies. These events tell us nothing about the use of the horse on the field of
battle.

Further reinforcing the case for the battlefield use of the horse, as well as
confirming the place of the Vikings, although by this stage we are looking at
organised state forces, specifically the Anglo-Danish, within the mainstream of
continental warfare, we turn to William of Poitiers and the Bayeux Tapestry.

Neither of these sources have any problem with Harold's participation in, or indeed his ability to participate in, William's Breton campaign.

Finally, with Harold, we turn to the Battle of Stamford Bridge. In many ways, the use of the horse by the English in the events prior to what turned out to be the second battle of the campaign of 1066 was highly conventional in that, as with Harold's earlier Welsh expedition, it fulfilled its everyday strategic mobility role. The problem arises in that in one of the most detailed, and certainly the best known, description of the battle, namely that contained in the *Heimskringla* of Snorri Sturluson, the Anglo-Danish use of cavalry is described in such a way as to elevate it to a pivotal position, while at the same time sounding remarkably like a slightly later and far more famous engagement. *Heimskringla* was written in the thirteenth century, thus the criticism that is usually levelled, namely that Snorri confused the events of Hastings and Stamford Bridge, is cogent. *Heimskringla* does not, however, stand alone; equally detailed accounts of the battle occur in the *Morkinskinna* and in the *Fagrskinna*, although they also date to the early thirteenth century and thus present the same transmission of information problems as Sturluson's work. Leaving these problems to one side for a minute, it must needs be admitted that with the exception of the 'feigned retreats', the description of the battle in these sources does not exceed the bounds of possibility. As for the use of a mounted force to pin and harass the Norwegians, this should be seen as a plausible tactic and certainly the sort of thing that would have been known and understood by Harold, and for that matter the Anglo-Danish military elite as a whole. The subject of the 'feigned retreats' is problematic and dependant upon context, for the Byzantine version of the manoeuvre differed from the Norman. Was it used at Stamford Bridge? Or was it a lucky battlefield occurrence given a post-facto rationalisation? Or, for that matter, is it a mistake in our later source material? Given the current state of the evidence, it is impossible to say. As for a mounted contingent at Stamford Bridge, well it remains a possibility that a part of Harold II's host remained horsed in order to pin and contain the enemy. However, given the dearth of information in our contemporary sources, little can be said other than that it remains a possibility, albeit a feasible one.

The evidence, such as there is, has therefore led Hooper to conclude that mounted combat took place 'mainly in skirmishes and pursuits rather than in pitched battles'. Although Hooper does not rule out the use of mounted contingents in pitched battles, he does believe that the Anglo-Saxons usually dismounted and formed a shield wall. There is no evidence to either positively support or refute this proposition, and the use of mounted contingents in pitched battles, therefore, remains a possibility.

Hooper's arguments concerning the concerning the Anglo-Saxons also fit the Vikings. Given the Vikings' obvious ability in raid, pursuit and rout, coupled with the Bayeux Tapestry's support for the fact that England's Anglo-Danish warrior aristocracy were a part of the European mainstream, it is probable that they at times deployed tactically diverse units on the battlefield, and that cavalry (in the broadest sense of the word and remembering initial definitions) were a part of the tactical repertoire of their armies, particularly given the Vendel background as well the continental influences. What may, especially in the first Viking age, have reduced their ability to field mounted contingents and engage in the mounted pursuit of defeated enemies was the need to acquire horses. Once armies started to overwinter, the ability to obtain horses rose dramatically. Prior to this point it was not an important part of their tactical repertoire, as the longship provided all the strategic mobility they required. Only once they started to wage a campaign of land-based warfare and ultimately conquest and settlement did the horse, with its dual role of transport and fighting platform, become more important. Little should be read into the absence of Anglo-Danish cavalry at the Battle of Hastings. Rather, we should see this as a case of 'horses for courses', or deployment to suit the tactical situation. At Hastings, surprise having failed, the position from Harold's point of view was better suited to infantry. Equally, Harold was undoubtedly wise in not allowing any of his horse to engage their, if not necessarily numerically superior, better opponents.

ARCHERY

Archaeologically, although we lack anything comparable to the earlier great continental bog deposits, finds from princely boat graves of Ladeby, Gokstad and Oseberg, along with finds from other, less exalted warrior graves, show that the Vikings, unsurprisingly, followed European practice and used the longbow. Of course, the problem lies in reconciling the lone Anglo-Danish archer in the Bayeux Tapestry with the contradictory literary and the scant archaeological evidence.

Norwegian laws of the twelfth and thirteenth century, which were derived from and are believed to reflect earlier Viking practice, required freemen who owed military service to bring, among other weapons, a bow when mustered for war. Meanwhile, the appearance of the bow as a weapon of war in Skaldic verse shows that it was not considered entirely unheroic. However, the busy bows at Maldon in 991 affected the outcome of the battle not at all, and this should caution us against assigning too important a role to Viking archery. As for the bow in later Norwegian laws, such provisions were probably more concerned with the limited naval warfare of the Viking Age than with the art of war on land in that period. The Vikings seemed to prefer to settle matters with the heroic ideal of close-order infantry combat, and thus they, most probably for similar reasons, placed little reliance on archers. The one obvious archery success story of the period was of course that of the Norman bowmen at Hastings. Yet in this most famous of cases, we are looking at something rather atypical.

William's expedition to England staked all on success, and in order to help secure the desired outcome he, William, recruited as many followers/mercenaries/ adventurers to his cause as possible. Thus, although it is impossible to put accurate figures on the number of bowmen (longbow and crossbow) present in the Duke's army, it is fair to say that the lure of the wealth of one of the richest kingdoms in Europe allowed William to exploit men's greed and as a consequence field a larger force of archers than was normal for a man in his position. As to where all these archers came from, well that is explained by the different tactical situation present on the continent as opposed to Anglo-Danish England. Or in other words: castles.

Castles were primarily secure bases, designed and located in order to allow armoured, mounted forces to control areas of land. In the attack and defence of such fortifications, archers played a vital role. Conversely, in lands where siege warfare was at best peripheral, then the role, presence and numbers of archers may have equally been reduced. Also, at Hastings we remember that the battle lasted all day and that the issue was decided as much by the archers' attritional shooting as by the (un)lucky death of Harold II as the day waned. What of the Welsh? Davies, in his 2004 study *Welsh Military Institutions 633–1283*, does not consider the bow to be a weapon of war in Wales until the Anglo-Norman period. Prior to this point in time, it appears to have been used solely in the hunt.

Where then does all of this leave Viking military archery? While there is an undoubted thread of military archery running through the whole of the Viking period, it appears that, at least in England, or rather Britain, the bow's contribution to the warfare of the day was rather limited, particularly when contrasted with its later successes. The arrow-storms of the later medieval period, of Agincourt, Towton, Crécy, etc., etc. have cast a long shadow. Equally, the success of the Norman archers at Hastings, coupled with the knowledge that Harold II deployed archers at Stamford Bridge, has led to the question – why were they not present, or not present in great numbers, at Hastings? The usual answer, that they were the poorest members of the *fyrd*, lacked horses and could not move as rapidly and were thus left behind on the march south, not only smacks of convenience but also rather ignores their rapid march north. A more probable answer to the question of whether the archers who fought at Stamford Bridge also fought at Hastings is yes, but in the former battle only a small number of archers fought on both sides, while in the latter battle the small contingent of Anglo-Danish archers were outnumbered by their opposite numbers on the other side. Why? Part of the why lies in the Anglo-Viking heroic tradition, and part lies in the Hellenistic period and the armies of the successor states.

The bow is not, and was not, a heroic weapon; a useful weapon certainly, but heroic – not really. Even in Homer's vision of the late Mycenaean world, the skill of Paris is not regarded as highly as Hector and Achilles' ability to deal out death at close quarters, and while most people's memory of the end of the *Odyssey* is of Odysseus stringing his great bow, the slaughter of the suitors really gets underway when he dons helmet and takes up shield and spear. Indeed, the end of the *Odyssey* provides an object lesson in heroic archery – the well-trained warrior should know how to use a bow, and the bow certainly had a use in certain stages, particularly the opening stages, of battle, but the real killing was done up close with spear and sword.

Despite all the sophistication of the Hellenistic warfare, missile troops played a small part in the battles of the day. The reason is simple and it applies equally to the Viking period and accounts for the Viking and Anglo-Saxon ambivalence towards, and decision not to raise or field, large numbers of archers. For, to put it quite simply, archers were a fragile element in the battle line. From all the evidence, it appears that the shield was a more than adequate defence against the archery of the day. Archers were also unable to withstand a determined assault by infantry and cavalry. As a consequence, they were confined to the periphery and the main killing was done by the other arms.

6

The Place of Slaughter

The place of slaughter, so reminiscent of Homer, is the brutally evocative phrase used by the Anglo-Saxon Chronicle to describe the battlefield. Yet although the popular image of the Vikings is one of a warrior culture, we still do not view the field of battle as their milieu. Rather, Vikings raid from the sea. Even this very phrase – Vikings raid from the sea – is in itself reminiscent of the Anglo-Saxon's poetic maxims:

> An earl belongs on a charger's back; a mounted troop ride in regular array and the foot solider must stand firm.

Maxims I

In this context the Vikings as sea-raiders fit, and in this context the Vikings are generally perceived. This is, however, unsurprisingly, too simplistic a view. The Viking period stretches from the eighth century AD to the eleventh century AD, and throughout the whole of this period we see them engaged in a variety of military activities against a number of enemies. The scale of their expeditions was not static, nor indeed was their motivation; indeed, the beginning of the age saw them as looters of Christian property while the end of it saw them as holy crusaders, spreading the word of God.

Thus, in martial terms, while they were indeed sea-raiders, it is too simplistic to view them solely in this light. We see, alongside their infamous attacks on coastal monasteries and settlements, mounted parties pillaging inland, great armies set on conquest and settlement, sieges in which the Vikings were sometimes the besiegers and sometimes the besieged, and merciless naval actions. They also acted as holy warriors, spreading the word of God to the pagans. Since they travelled widely, to four continents, they racked up an impressive collection of enemies, victims and allies.

While we do not, of course, know of every small skirmish, we are in a good position to enumerate a long list of battles and raids. However, that is at times all it can be – a list. Contemporary sources are quite happy to tell us of outcomes and indeed go so far as to state who had 'possession of the place of slaughter', or in other words who won. They very rarely go into any detail and even where they do, they certainly do not provide the level of information that we as historians demand of them. This is, of course, as discussed in chapter two, hardly surprising, for the authors of the various poems, annals and chronicles had a different worldview and were pursuing different agendas to ourselves. We thus end up, as Griffith called it, *tactical snippetting*, taking pieces of information from here and there in order to build up a picture or image of how exactly the Vikings conducted a raid, fought a particular battle, what techniques they used or at least had available to them when conducting a siege. This is less than ideal but, to paraphrase Field Marshal Lord Kitchener, we must make history as we must: not as we would like.

RAIDING

The quintessential Viking activity: dragon-prowed ships crashing up the beach, armoured men jumping ashore with fear and terror going before them. The sack of the monastery at Lindisfarne in Northumberland in AD 793 as recorded in the Anglo-Saxon Chronicle, although not the opening act of the Viking Age, is certainly one of the best remembered and has in many ways acted as a leitmotif for the whole period. This action sent shock waves throughout Western Christendom. Alcuin, at the court of Charlemagne, was horrified. Yet for all their undoubted fame as raiders, how much do we actually know about the tactics employed in such raids? Griffith paints a detailed picture of the techniques employed but his description, if not pure conjecture, is simply an exercise in probability. He himself states in the preface to his work that he is applying 'modern military analysis' and by extension modern infantry tactics to the Vikings' art of war. To a degree, this is valid: the Vikings form part of the continuum that is the Western way of war, which began in Archaic Greece and which extends to the modern Western armies of the present day. However, we see a change in tactics in the nineteenth century, and also in the twentieth century, which makes such comparisons harder to maintain. Although, of course, it could be argued that even if main battle tactics changed, small-unit raiding tactics remained pretty much static.

The theory for sacking a monastery would have seen an attacking force divided into four groups. One group, the smallest, would have stayed with the longships as a boat guard. A second group would string themselves out as a cordon to entrap the inhabitants and prevent their escape. In theory, this second group served two purposes: one was to prevent word of the attack reaching the outside world, thus preventing a possible counter-attack; the second, more mercenary, reason was to prevent valuables being carried or walking (potential slaves) away. The third group, the main group, attacked the target and behind them came the final, mopping-up group.

There is absolutely nothing wrong with this model – it is a textbook sack of a monastery/hall complex/small settlement – but, and there is of course a but, is it supported by the evidence?

The problem with testing the theory lies, as always, with what is probably best described as 'world view'. For the authors (or compilers) of the various annals and chronicles which are the best sources for the period not only had different priorities but also a different understanding of causality. We cynical postmodern people view monasteries as obvious, wealthy, soft targets, ripe for the picking; these factors, coupled with their locations on coasts and river systems, provided the rationale for their sacking. To Alcuin, the great Northumbrian scholar and teacher at the court of Charlemagne, however, the sack of Lindisfarne in AD 793 was searing – God's wrath on a sinful people. Horrifying, justifiable, yet, presciently, merely the beginning:

> What should be expected for other places, when the divine judgement has not spared this Holy place?

> Alcuin to Ethelred, King of Northumbria

The Anglo-Saxon Chronicle is equally shocked. However, it reads the signs before the event and in its stark language, it makes no judgement.

> Here terrible portents came about in the land of Northumbria, and grievously afflicted the people: there were tremendous flashes of lightning, and fiery dragons were seen flying in the sky, and there immediately followed a great famine, and after that in that same year the raiding of the heathen miserably devastated God's church in Lindisfarne island by looting and slaughter.

> Anglo-Saxon Chronicle (F ms.), AD 793

The entry in the E ms. for the Anglo-Saxon Chronicle is practically identical and this is the level of detail we usually get in the chronicles and annals of the period. Paucity of detail is not confined to the Anglo-Saxon sources. The Royal Frankish Annals (see, for example, the entry for AD 820) are equally brief, as indeed are the Annals of Clonmacnoise, to name but one of the Irish annals. A rare tactical detail occurs in the AD 873 entry of the Annals of Fulda. Here we are told that one Rudolf first sent emissaries ahead demanding tribute, an action incidentally which we see again in the later Anglo-Saxon poem *The Battle Of Maldon*. Rudolf, upon hearing that his demands would not be met,

> swore that after all the males had been killed the women and children with all their moveable wealth should be taken into captivity.

> Annals of Fulda, 873

Even here, though, we are seeing more a general statement of intent than a detailed description of a plan. The Anglo-Saxon Chronicle's (A ms) recording of the events leading up to the Battle of Maldon points to another aspect of sea raiding, part of which one could view as planned but which could easily be a result of necessity.

According to the A ms. of the Anglo-Saxon Chronicle, the Vikings, prior to their attack on Maldon, first went to

> Folkstone, and raided round about it, and then went from there to Sandwich and so from there to Ipswich and overran all that, and so to Maldon.

As a strategy, this makes perfect sense. The attack on Folkstone is followed by the short, swift move up to the coast to Sandwich; after Sandwich, Kent is left behind and the raiders are in East Anglia, sacking Ipswich. They then turn back south again rather than continuing north, with the planned attack on Maldon being designed to throw the defenders off their scent. The whole thing, the short jump north followed by the larger one, which is in turn followed by the move back south, is all, as far as we are concerned, part of the rationale of raiding.

The strategic mobility of sea raiders and their ability to stay one step ahead of a polity's defensive force is notorious and, in the context of these islands, is one of the reasons behind the third-century AD rebellion of Carausius. Thus if Rome, with all its power and for all its control of both sides of the Channel, could not stop similar pirate raids, what chance had Anglo-Saxon England, Frankia, or any of the other areas prayed upon by the Vikings for that matter? Of course, behind our neat military interpretation of the events of AD 991 there lies another factor – namely the weather.

The Viking longship was a sailing ship. It could, of course, also be propelled by oars, but its speed and strategic mobility lay in its sail, and as a consequence it was dependant upon the wind and the weather. This is not to say that our neat military interpretation of the events of AD 991 is wrong – rather, it needs some modification. Maldon, as a town and a mint, was an obvious target; let us not take that away from it. However, so were many other places. The Vikings, on leaving Ipswich, may well have planned to attack Maldon next; equally, and flexibility is all ways a part of this sort of warfare, Maldon may have been one of a list of targets, with the final choice being driven more by the wind than by the commanders of the raiding force. Maldon was however, as we know, attacked, although the raid, as we will see, from the Viking point of view miscarried and the result lies not within raiding; rather, it is within the purview of battle.

> And the heathen men stayed in Thanet over the winter.
>
> Anglo-Saxon Chronicle (E ms) AD 851 [850]

In raiders' terms, the fact that Vikings chose to overwinter in this country marks a significant change in this type of activity. Raiding from the sea does not preclude the possibility that those activities can and will to some degree be pushed inland. All of the Viking targets would have given them access to horses, and as the boat-graves from Vendel and Valsgärde show, pre-Viking Scandinavia and, as a consequence, Viking Scandinavia, was ruled by a horse-riding warrior elite. The very people who went a-Viking were as at home on a horse as they were on board a longship.

The problem, of course, with sacking say a monastery and then using that as a springboard to raid some distance inland is that you increase your chance of being caught, albeit usually on the way back.

Coastal targets, particularly soft ones such as a monastery, were the easiest to attack; the sea provided a rapid strategic highway. In order to penetrate the interior, and thus increase the number of available targets, the Vikings resorted to two solutions. Travel by water was, at that time, faster than by land. Thus the great of rivers of Europe, particularly the Thames, Seine and Guadalquivir, which gave access to such rich entrepôts as London, Paris and Seville, were all used by the Vikings. Many other waterways were also used; for example, in this country the Humber and the Ouse gave them access to York, while the Tyne laid the Venerable Bede's old monastery of St Paul's at Jarrow open to sack. Thus, until comparatively recently, waterways proved to be a country's most effective highways. However, not all places are accessible by water.

Today, the horse is seen as an old-fashioned method of transport. Yet even as late as the Second World War, the horse still played a vital part. Nor should we view this role simply as logistical. The German army employed 700,000 horses in its invasion of Russia, and both sides (Russia and Germany) employed cavalry in a reconnaissance role.

In the Viking Age the horse provided both sides, raiders and raided, with strategic mobility on land. On top of this, while Vikings and Anglo-Saxons could, as seen here, fight on horseback to some degree, some Viking opponents were far more proficient tactically on horseback. The Byzantines and the Islamic world had a cavalry tradition built upon the two great empires of the Ancient World, Rome and Persia. Meanwhile, the Carolingians and Ottonians were building a mounted tradition which we now view as the precursor to the medieval knight.

Horses, as well as providing a speedy means of plundering an enemy's territory, were also an end in their own right. In AD 866 [865], the Anglo-Saxon Chronicle A ms. tells us that the East Anglians bought peace with horses. Appeasement kept East Anglia safe from the 'Great Raiding-Army' for the time being at least. A new year and a new campaigning season revealed the purpose behind the horses. In AD 867 [866], the 'Great Raiding-Army' moved swiftly north thanks to the horses. Taking advantage of the political turmoil which embroiled the Kingdom of Northumbria (it had at this time two rival monarchs), the Vikings captured York. The subsequent slaughter, both inside and outside the city, saw the death of both kings and the end of Northumbria as an independent Anglo-Saxon kingdom.

By sea, but particularly by land, raiders were at their most detectable and thus their most vulnerable after they had hit their target, for at that point they became visible. They appeared, so to speak, on the defenders' radar and were potentially, provided that forces were available, open to counter-attack. This is most famously seen in the late third century AD. Carausius (the future usurper), according to the fourth-century authors Eutropius and S. Aurelius Victor, charged with protecting what we know as the Saxon Shore, essentially the coast of south-east Britain and northern France, scored a great number of successes against Saxon and Frankish pirates. He caught, so our sources tell us, many barbarians, but only after they had struck. The reasons for this are, quite simply, that the elements of surprise and uncertainty are now gone; equally, the raiding force is potentially reduced by casualties and slowed by the necessity to transport booty, the purpose in many cases of the raid. They are thus easier to find and easier to defeat. Of course, on rare occasions, and Maldon is the best example of this, the raiders were intercepted before they hit their intended target.

Before leaving the subject of raiding we must needs consider the Viking reputation for perpetrating atrocities. How brutal were the Vikings?

The simplest explanation would be to say that they were brutal men in a brutal age. But is it really as simple as that? The sack of Lindisfarne sent shock waves across Western Europe, but the reporters of that and similar events, the authors of the Anglo-Saxon Chronicle, the Annals of Fulda, the Annals of Clonmacnoise, the letters of Alcuin, etc. all had a vested interest in decrying this, indeed any, attack on the Church. The Vikings were not the first and would not be the last to be tarred with the brush of brutality. Nevertheless, such attacks did occur and terror is a very effective weapon; of course, your viewpoint is very much determined by which side you are on. Let us not forget that Joshua (6.21) had every living thing in Jericho put to the sword, while McGlynn in his recent book *By Sword & Fire* has shown that the 'Age of Chivalry' was not so chivalrous after all. Equally, the punishments routinely meted out as exemplars by the locally constituted authorities show that in many ways the sanctioned use of violence was rather prosaic. Halsall had argued that the Vikings were not *per se* crueller than anyone else; rather, they were simply doing it their own way. Every age seeks to improve upon its predecessor; monasteries, as we have already observed, were soft targets and this fact was not simply a feature of the Viking Age. Bishop Wilfred was critical of that good Christian King Ecgfrith who had, in AD 684, sent a force against the Irish which, in the pursuit of their mission, 'wretchedly abused and burned God's churches'. (Anglo-Saxon Chronicle, E ms.)

The Vikings undoubtedly committed atrocities. Violence and brutality are at times vital constituents of warfare and the Vikings employed them to the full. It is arguable that they were more violent than the warriors who had gone before and less so than those that followed. The lack of exact details leaves the whole question open to question.

NAVAL WARFARE

Named by tradition as the founder of the Royal Navy, Alfred the Great's claim to this title largely rests upon the events of AD 897 [896] as recorded by the Anglo-Saxon Chronicle A ms, when, according to the writer of the Chronicle, he ordered the building of new, larger warships. Alfred's 'Great' new ships were in action the same year against a Danish force off the south coast of England. Yet before we get carried away with stirring tales of daring-do, we must remember that these were not warships in the sense that we now commonly understand. A number of ship forms exist from the Viking Age, with the Skuldelev ships from Roskilde Fjord being among the best preserved. As a result of this and other finds, we are able to distinguish two distinct types of vessel, trading ships and warships. It is this latter type for which the Vikings are most famous, yet their warships, or longships as they are more commonly called, were in effect little more than swift landing craft.

Vegetius' earlier conception of Roman warships is more like our vision of such vessels in that (*Epitome Rei Militaris* IV.44) he recommends the use of ship-borne torsion artillery. Meanwhile, the Vikings' contemporary opponents the Byzantine Empire deployed dromōns, or battleships with raised fighting platforms and a *siphōn* or Greek fire flamethrowers. Equally, if we look to the twelfth century, just beyond the very end of the Viking Age, we see the rise of the cog. Primarily a merchantman, the cog's design, with its high freeboard and ability to add 'castles' (raised, crenellated fighting platforms) fore and aft, as well as at the masthead (a topcastle), made it better suited to naval warfare in northern waters. If ship design was changing by the twelfth century, the same could not be said for naval warfare.

> The same year King Alfred sent a raiding ship-army from Kent into East Anglia. Immediately they came to the mouth of the Stour, then they met 16 ships of the Vikings and fought against them, and got all the ships, and killed the men.
>
> Anglo-Saxon Chronicle, E ms., AD 885 [884]

Encounters such as the one above, and indeed others listed in the Anglo-Saxon Chronicle, were in two respects very similar to most naval battles fought throughout the whole of human history. Firstly, it took place in coastal waters; very rarely do such battles take place far out to sea. Secondly, although Alfred's force was in all probability looking for the Vikings, the meeting was undoubtedly more a result of luck than judgement. In a later age, Nelson twice criss-crossed the Mediterranean searching for fleets he knew existed. He eventually, successfully, brought them both to battle at Aboukir Bay and Trafalgar. But even almost a thousand years after the events described in the Anglo-Saxon Chronicle, finding and engaging the enemy at sea remained a remarkably chancy and uncertain process.

We are in some ways less well informed about such battles than about their land equivalents; in other ways, however, there is less to tell. Thjodolfr Arnorsson's partially preserved skaldic poem of the Battle of the River Nissa, which was fought on 9 August 1062 between Harold Hardrada of Norway and Sveinn of Denmark, does at least describe the opening of the battle. The tactics may not have been universal, although there is nothing either unusual or radical about them. Indeed, given the similarity between naval and land battles, we should not be surprised that clashes at sea began with an exchange of missiles.

> The valiant King of Uppland drew his bow all night; the lord caused arrows to shower against the white shields [of Demark]. The blood-drenched points inflicted wounds upon the mail-shirted men, where arrows lodged in shields; the volley of spears from the dragon [longship] increased.
>
> Thjodolfr Arnorsson, 'The Battle of the River Nissa', from *Sexstefja*, 10

The preceding verse tells us that the shield wall was formed along the bulwark. Thus the opening missile storm: first arrows, then javelins and spears. Ships, and thus battles at sea, were won or lost by the ability to board and take enemy vessels. In order to board, a gap, or gaps, must be made in the enemy shield wall, which was, because of the fewer men involved and the cramped space, one or possibly two men deep. The opening missile exchange was designed to, at best, breach but most likely thin out the opposing ship's crew. Breaches would most probably be made when the vessels came together and the two sides engaged each other in hand-to-hand combat.

We forget at times how costly naval warfare can be, with slaughter at sea being eclipsed by, at times, less costly land engagements. The dead of Cannae and the first day of the Somme are well recorded, yet at Salamis in 480 BC some 40,000 Persians drowned in the warm waters of the Aegean, with a similar number of Christians and Muslims perishing at Lepanto in AD 1571.

The problem lies not so much in the fact that such engagements were fought under oars, but rather in that boarding was, in the Vikings' case, the only weapon. A ship was safe when it was cleared. To safely clear a ship, it was best to either kill or force overboard its crew, for unlike on land, you cannot simply run away. Battles at sea in this period were a grim, dangerous, desperate business.

This is to some extent implied by the Anglo-Saxon Chronicle when it speaks of all being killed. Thjodolfr Arnorsson, in his description of the Battle of the River Nissa, is more explicit, in that Harald's force cleared 'Sveinn's men's splendid ships', sending all the men to hell in the process. Sveinn, by a miracle, escaped.

The possibility exists, and is described in some Sagas, that in large fleet engagements one side, the defending side, would secure their ships together to create a larger, more stable fighting platform, as well as a solid, impenetrable formation. Given that this happened at Sluys in AD 1340, we should not, as naval warfare had changed little by this period, dismiss the possibility out of hand. As on land, once the two sides came together, the missile exchange need not necessarily have stopped; the spear, however, now became the primary weapon. Its length and thus reach made it ideally suited to killing across the gunwales. Once the spear had done its job, namely killing and creating a gap, the tricky and dangerous task of moving from one bobbing, unstable platform (your own longship) over to another bobbing, unstable platform (the enemy's longship) must be attempted.

Boarding, no matter when in history it has been attempted, is a difficult and dangerous process, complicated by the fact that the vessels are not only moving but that their sides are unlikely to match perfectly. Indeed, Alfred the Great's new, bigger ships with their higher gunwales were specifically designed to make it harder for an enemy to board. Equally, they may also have made it harder for their own crew to board an enemy vessel. If you misjudged and went overboard (particularly while wearing armour) then you were very likely to drown and while you are trying to cross, your erstwhile opponents are trying at weapon's point to stop you. At this point, the spear would have become an encumbrance; sword and axe would now be used to 'clear' the enemy's deck. The possibility also exists, not simply among the Rus, but also among the Vikings who had had dealings with them, that maces, which were a feature of both Steppe and Byzantine warfare, were also used in this last, desperate phase of fighting.

Once boarding had occurred, the hand-to-hand combat would reach fever pitch, becoming,

> A bloody and murderous battle. [For] sea fights are always fiercer than fights on land, because retreat and flight are impossible. Every man is obliged to hazard his life and hope for success, relying on his own personal bravery and skill.

> Froissart, Book 1

Depending, of course, on the size of the engagement and the number of vessels involved, a successful crew might have to clear more than one enemy vessel.

To the victor the spoils. There would, as in all actions, be bodies to strip. However, the main prize was the ship. The vessel itself was a valuable, prestige item and in a culture which stressed boarding and did not attempt sinking, at the end of an engagement the captured longships would have suffered minimal damage and be perfectly capable of being sailed or towed away by the victorious side.

SIEGE

Siege warfare is viewed as very much a medieval activity. Alongside Jerusalem in AD 1099, Chateau Gaillard in AD 1203–04 and Constantinople itself in AD 1453, the great warriors of the age, men such as Henry II of England, his son Richard I, and Philip Augustus of France, made their name not in the field of battle but rather in the field of siege warfare. Equally, French victory in the Hundred Years War came not on the battlefield but from the systematic reduction of English strongholds. Yet for all this, it is not an activity that is generally associated with the Vikings. By its very nature siege warfare is slow and methodical, the very antithesis of the swift-striking sea raiding with which we commonly and exclusively associate the Vikings, and in this image we would be wrong for the Vikings were at times both besieged and besiegers. In the former role they constructed defensive field fortifications; in the latter they threw up lines of circumvallation. They besieged London, Paris and Constantinople, in the process deploying siege machines and artillery. Siege warfare was very much a medieval activity and in this respect the Vikings were very medieval.

Christiansen argues that the spade was a vital part of the Vikings' armoury and to some extent that is true. However, its value was dependent upon circumstance. Field or temporary fortifications were undoubtedly a feature of Scandinavian warfare before the first Viking Age; however, at the opening of this period they were not seen. The reason for this is very simple and straightforward – they were not seen because they were not needed. The swift raiding phase of the first Viking age did not require the attackers to protect themselves in such a manner. The picture changes when the raiders started to overwinter in enemy territory. Once this occurred, a secure base was needed. Initially islands such as Thanet and Sheppey were used – both were defendable without the need to engage in the labour of fortress building.

Such sites were, however, not always available. In AD 871, so Asser tells us in his *Life of King Alfred*, at Reading in Berkshire the Viking army fortified (with rampart and gate) an area of land between the rivers Thames and Kennet. Today, we can stand at the confluence of the two rivers and look towards what was the Viking camp, although we cannot with any certainty delimit it. We are on better ground, so to speak, at Repton in Derbyshire. Here in AD 873 a Viking host constructed a great 'u'-shaped bank and ditch stretching south from the River Trent, in the process incorporating St Wystan's church into their defensive system.

At Repton an existing building was utilised as part of the defensive perimeter. At Nijmegen in AD 880–881 the Vikings, so we are told in The Annals of Fulda,

> Put a strong rampart and wall around Nimwegen [Nijmegen] and made themselves winter quarters in the King's palace. Louis came against them with a strong army and returned without having accomplished much, because of the hardship of the winter and the strength of the fortifications.

Viking fortifications were not always so securely held. In 921 [917], according to the Anglo-Saxon Chronicle A ms, King Edward besieged and took the Viking stronghold at Tempsford. Following the rules of war, Edward slew a great many of the defenders. The siege of Tempsford took place in the summer, so unlike at Nijmegen the defenders did not have General Winter to aid them. As well as creating new defences, the Vikings also utilised (not always successfully) existing, albeit at times abandoned, settlements. Thus we see them occupying, among other locations, Waltham, York, Cirencester and the ruins of Chester. The Anglo-Saxons, Carolingians and Ottonians of necessity were forced to besiege

Viking fortifications, whatsoever and wheresoever they may be. The Vikings were neither so obliged to reciprocate, nor would they in the main have seen the need to do it, although they did occasionally indulge in such behaviour.

In AD 917 the Vikings attacked the strongholds of Towcester and Wigingamere to no avail (Anglo-Saxon Chronicle, A ms, 921 [917]). Such attacks were not, as was usually the case, motivated by a desire for loot and reward but by a desire to curtail the power and unifying proclivities of Wessex.

Generally however, the Vikings, if they chose to besiege a target, chose a rich one. Thus, and they could be very persistent in their pursuit of victory, Viking forces besieged London, York, Paris; even the great city of Constantinople was not immune from attack.

Comparing the sieges of Paris in AD 885–6 and London in AD 1016, we do not see an increase in technical sophistication; rather, and leaving aside the fact that both sieges failed, what we do see is an increase in organisational sophistication. This latter change is undoubtedly a reflection not only of the passage of time between the two sieges, but also concomitantly of the nature of the forces conducting each siege.

According to Abbo of Saint-Germain-des-Prés' poem the *Bella Parisiacae Urbis*, the Viking forces which attacked Paris in AD 885–886 were a pretty disorganised bunch. However, leaving this obvious biased hyperbole aside, what we do see is that the Vikings used a range of techniques to attack and breach the defences.

Some sort of *testudo* formation was used to allow the Vikings to approach and attempt to fill in the city's ditches, as were ox-hide-covered missile shields, or cats to give them their medieval nickname. Equally, to subdue the defenders we see the use of fireships, while a metal-tipped, wheeled battering ram was also employed. As well as arrows, spears and javelins, both sides hurled stones at each other. Hand-thrown stones are a very effective weapon, and Abbo also informed us that the Frankish defenders of Paris constructed a traction trebuchet. It is less clear if the Vikings employed such simple, yet effective, artillery pieces.

Before turning to the Vikings' organisational failure at Paris, we must first address the question of the *testudo*. Part of the problem lies with the fact that the *testudo* was a very specific Roman military formation and authors, both Frankish and Anglo-Saxon, attempted to display their erudition by using a smattering of Latin technical terms, at times incorrectly. This is particularly prevalent in the military sphere. However, having said that, a *testudo*-like formation is entirely consistent with troops under missile attack approaching enemy fortifications. The potential organisational failure of the siege, and we should not take Abbo's biased descriptions too literally, lies in the overall direction of the siege and may result not from a lack of will but from a lack of manpower on the Vikings' part. Starvation is an essential part of siege warfare.

The Vikings' failure to completely invest Paris did not auger well for the success of the siege, as it allowed the Franks to be reinforced and provisioned as the siege progressed. This failure on the Vikings' part may have resulted from a lack of men. It could also be the result of the fact that none of the groups, or more specifically the commanders of the Viking groups, which made up the attacking force wished to guard an unglamorous and unheroic section of the siege works. Divided command, coupled with this heroic ideal, does not sit well with siege warfare, which of its very nature required a methodical approach. The conduct of sieges is notoriously difficult and as a result it should come as no surprise that the Viking sieges of London in AD 1016, like the earlier attacks on Paris, ended in failure. The first assault in AD 1016 was by far from the most sophisticated. According to the Anglo-Saxon Chronicle D ms, the Vikings 'bedyked the town around so that no one could get in or out, and regularly attacked the town'. These lines of circumvallation may well have paid off given time. However, Viking assaults on the English fortifications failed and the new King, Edmund, arrived with an army and, driving the Danes away, he raised the siege.

Returning to London later the same year, the Vikings, it would appear, attempted unsuccessfully to escalade the town, attacking simultaneously by land and water. This new assault followed its predecessor and again resulted in failure. Leaving aside the failures, the most important part is that at London, unlike Paris, we have moved away from bands, ship's companies coming together to form a larger force. The Anglo-Saxon Chronicle falls back to the shorthand of 'The Raiding-Army', but what we are seeing is in fact is a royal army.

Cnut may not have had a kingdom as such but he would have exercised authority after the manner of his late father, Swein of Denmark. Thus, with one overall controlling will, works such a line of circumvallation become far more feasible.

Failure was not always a feature of Viking sieges. Their seizure of York in AD 867 [866] (Anglo-Saxon Chronicle A ms) was, however, facilitated by the fact that 'in those days the city did not yet have firm and secure walls.' (Asser, *Life of King Alfred*, 27)

The defenders of Paris and London prevailed; York may have capitulated without siege in AD 886, as it was to again two hundred years later in the face of Harald Hardrada's victorious army. What, however, the former defeats illustrate, and they were chosen because they are comparatively well described in contemporary sources, is that the Vikings understood and employed a variety of techniques. Thus, aspects of warfare not necessarily associated with the Vikings, such as lines of circumvallation, siege machinery and engines, were actually part of their repertoire, as they were for the Franks and the Anglo-Saxons. Thus, in this, as in other areas, the Vikings were very much a part of the European mainstream.

BATTLE

Let us go ashore, before warriors and large armies learn that the English homelands are being traversed with shields: let us be brave in battle, brandish spears and hurl them; great numbers of the English flee before our swords.

Liðsmannaflokkr

If we take the later seventh-century laws of Ine as a starting point, the forces engaged in the battles listed in the Anglo-Saxon Chronicle were armies. Ine 13.1 states that anything over thirty-five, basically a boat crew, was a *here*, or army. However, beyond this detail, particularly in the Anglo-Saxon Chronicle, is rather thin on the ground. We are told that one side or another had 'possession of the place of slaughter', the Chronicle's grim, poetic name for the battlefield. Also, despite popular views to the ceremony, the Vikings were not all-conquering.

Nor is the Anglo-Saxon Chronicle alone in this regard. The various Frankish and Irish chronicles, histories and annals are equally content, in the main, to simply list that a battle occurred and that one side was victorious. There is also quite often a phrase about 'great slaughter' and this, combined with the Anglo-Saxon Chronicle's naming of the battlefield as the 'place of slaughter', could so very easily be dismissed as simply the use of stock phrases. However, we should not so readily dismiss such phrases, for at some point one side would collapse and attempt to flee. Order would dissolve, serried ranks would become a mob and the losing side would attempt to escape the victors. The pursuit is when the true slaughter would begin, but we will look at this in more detail below where we consider the Battle of Brunanburh.

Of course, we should not expect the various annals and chronicles to provide the sort of detail we want; that, after all, was not their purpose. However, they do, as we saw in the previous chapter, provide some tactical details and we are not completely bereft of information when it comes to some of the great battles of the age.

At Ashdown in AD 871, the Vikings formed two shield walls side-by-side at the top of a hill (Asser, *Life of King Alfred*, 37–39), yet despite the apparent advantage of numbers and position they still went down to defeat. Brunanburh was a great battle, a truly complete victory the likes of which was probably not seen again in this country until the Battle of Stamford Bridge in AD 1066, and like the latter battle, the fruits of the victory of Brunanburh were similarly as fleeting and transient.

The best précis of events leading up to and subsequently following the battle itself are to be found in Clare Downham's recent work, *Viking Kings of Britain and Ireland*. The best description of the battle itself is in the celebratory poem which forms the Anglo-Saxon Chronicle entry for the year AD 937, the year of the battle. A highly entertaining, yet staggeringly fanciful description of the battle can be found in *Egil's Saga*. The Saga is a fun, enjoyable read, but not as a source for the Battle of Brunanburh. Its hazel-rod delimited, agreed battle-site is utter nonsense.

The battle was fought between an English force led by the King, Athelstan, and his brother Edmund, and a coalition of Vikings (from both England and Ireland) and Scots. The Vikings were led by Olaf Guðfriðsson, King of Dublin, and the Scots by Constantine, King of Alba. The site of the battle itself remains unknown and given the present state of the evidence, unknowable, despite much scholarly debate. The Anglo-Saxon Chronicle speaks of Dingesmere/Dyngesmere/

Dynigesmere/Dinnesmere, depending on which manuscript you are reading, while the Annals of Clonmacnoise 931 [=937] talks of the battle and 'great slaughter' 'on the plains of othlyn'. Until such time as one or both of these places can be located, the discussion regarding the battle's actual location will continue.

The battle itself cannot be described as a long, hard-fought engagement, yet still it lasted all day.

We cannot say for certain, other than in the morning, at what time the armies initially clashed, although, as will become apparent, it was probably quite early in the morning. As we will see when we look at the Battle of Maldon in AD 991, we are able to create a relative chronology, if not an absolute one. Thus at Brunanburh, Athelstan breaks the Scots and Viking shield wall very quickly (by line four of the poem), beginning the slaughter which would last all day:

> ... the field darkened with soldiers' blood, after in the morning-time the sun, that glorious star, bright candle of God, the Lord Eternal, glided over the depths, until the noble creature sank to rest.

Why the Vikings and Scots broke so quickly cannot be guessed. Battle is a very risky endeavour and can, as it did on this occasion, go spectacularly wrong for the losing side. How then, if the forces of Olaf and Constantine were defeated so quickly, did the battle last all day? Battles have phases and, while in all battles such phases can be identified, they varied in length within and between battles. The phases (and they can be given different names) are deployment, skirmishes and missile exchange, close to contact, close-order combat, collapse and finally pursuit. That final phase, the pursuit, dominated Brunanburh.

> All day long the West Saxons with mounted warriors pressed in the tracks of the hateful nation with mill-sharp blades severely hacked from behind those who had fled battle.

The battle did in effect last all day, but most of it was taken up with pursing and slaughtering a broken enemy. The Brunanburh poem is mostly concerned with death: the death of the raiding army and the death of its Scottish allies. It was viewed as the most complete, bloodiest victory since the coming of the Anglo-Saxons and this is hardly surprising, for very rarely are the victors of the shield wall clash in a position to pursue all through what, for the defeated, must have been a very long and harrowing day.

Great victories are very rarely decisive and the Battle of Brunanburh was no exception; two years later the Dublin Vikings re-conquered Northumbria, albeit temporarily. The pursuit of battle as a war-winning strategy was not simply a feature of the modern age. In AD 937 the Brunanburh protagonists pursued this course and we will see it again in the events of AD 1066. Not all battles were, however, so pre-planned. The best-recorded battle (apart from Hastings) came about as a result of luck and accident.

The fame of the Battle of Maldon rests upon the fact that it was the first great defeat of the Second Viking Age, and given that it occurred at the start of the renewal of Viking activity, it has at times been viewed by later commentators not only as a precursor to but also the reason behind Æthelred's future problems and failures. Coupled with this is the death of Byrhtnoth in the battle; despite subsequent criticism of his folly and arrogance, particularly in respect to his own command decisions, his loss at such a crucial time has been viewed as a serious blow to Æthelredian England. Finally, its fame rests upon the survival of some 325 lines of poetry. The poem, which we know as *The Battle of Maldon*, is incomplete; it lacks a beginning and an end, as well as a title. Yet for all that the poem, which was probably written just after the defeat, provides a realistic outline of the events of the engagement.

In the summer of the year 991, a Viking fleet ravaged the coast of England. Its first target, or victim, was Folkestone; it next attacked Sandwich. After Sandwich, well after Sandwich we see the real value of the warships of the period, namely strategic mobility. For the Vikings now left Kent and the South-East behind, turning their attention to East Anglia instead – they appeared suddenly at Ipswich. This type of warfare raiding, or (to coin a later medieval term) a sort of naval *chevauchée*, is predicated on speed, surprise and the avoidance of battle, and these factors account for the Vikings' decision to backtrack and attack Maldon. Equally, they have tended to be overlooked when considering the engagement which occurred outside Maldon, as indeed has the geography of Northey Island itself (far too much time has been spent staring at the causeway and in criticising Byrthnoth's *ofermod*).

The Vikings undoubtedly knew both Maldon and Northey Island and would have chosen the island as a landing site for two reasons. Firstly, the island is accessible only by boat or by the causeway at low tide; it thus provided the Vikings with a secure, easily guarded landing site for their ships. Secondly, importantly, Northey Island is a hill; thus, anyone landing on the eastern side of the island is nicely screened from Maldon by the hill which forms the western side of the island. Given this, we are able to tentatively reconstruct the Vikings' plan of attack, always bearing in mind that they were intending to raid and sack Maldon, not fight a pitched battle.

On the night of 10/11 August 991, the causeway at Northey Island was completely clear at 4.43 a.m. The Vikings would therefore have unstepped their masts at night, at sea, and then pulled upstream to Northey Island in the darkness, intent upon using the island itself to cover their landing. Crossing the causeway, probably even before it was completely clear, they would have purposed to take the sleepy defenders of Maldon at unawares. They would not have wanted to attack manned fortifications, for it is 'murdering' to attack across ditches and walls which have not been filled and breached in the face of a determined defence; far better to escalade a sleeping garrison. Certainly this was not without precedent, as night attacks by Vikings occurred at Bordeaux in 848 and at Chartres a decade later, in 858.

Yet for the Vikings their plan miscarried – they were seen and not only was their target forewarned, but a force was available to intercept them on landing. It is unlikely that their intentions were divined upon leaving Ipswich, as they would have been well out of sight of land before they turned south towards Maldon. Rather, they were probably spotted upon entering the Blackwater. Now, for the English we can see what can only be described as the first stroke of luck. Naval warfare is a decidedly tricky and chancy affair; even as late as the twentieth century the bringing together of two opposing fleets has proved well nigh impossible. Even Rome, for all its wealth, power and martial prowess, was unable to prevent or suppress Saxon piracy from the third century onwards. Carausius, the Roman official turned usurper, charged with the task of ending such raids, observed that it was far easier (indeed, it was at least possible) to intercept the pirates after the event rather than before it. Byrhtnoth's ability to bar the causeway we should therefore ascribe to luck rather than good judgement. Luck in that the Vikings were seen; luck in that not only did the intelligence reach Byrhtnoth in time, but also in that he was able to both interpret it correctly and be close enough to Maldon and Northey Island to allow him to act upon it. The one factor in all of this which does not rely upon luck is the fact that Byrhtnoth and his host were probably already assembled in this area as a result of the earlier raids.

The Vikings, on disembarking, pulled their ships up onto the flat east side of the island, arrayed themselves in their armour and, passing along the south-east side of Northey Island, shielded by the hill, they made their way to the causeway to await the tide. Yet to their surprise they found a most unwelcome sight – an English army. From the poem (and in this part of the chapter the poem, unless otherwise stated, is always *The Battle of Maldon*), lines 2–24, it appears that the English had themselves only just arrived and that the Vikings were able to watch as Byrhtnoth put his forces into array. Horses were sent to the rear and the shield wall formed. Byrhtnoth's advice, lines 18–21, on how to stand, how to hold the shield, was not, as has at times ludicrously been stated, on-the-spot training. Rather, it is the Maldon poet's echoing of the seventh-century BC Greek elegiast Tyrtaeus'

> Fear ye not a multitude of men, nor flinch, but let every man hold his shield straight towards the van.

We are seeing no more than the mantra of Western close-order infantry combat – stand straight, stand steady, look to your front.

For the Vikings, this turn of events would have been unexpected and unwelcome. Battles are dreadfully risky affairs which can leave even the victors exhausted and badly damaged. Therefore, attempting guile, the poem (lines 25–6) sees the raiders asking for and, understandably, being refused tribute. Now, this section of the poem is easy to view in the light of later payments – yet more fundamental is the assumption that at this point battle was inevitable. Why was this so? Yes, we know that a battle did take place, but everyone has been so hung up on Byrhtnoth's generalship and, of course, his *ofermod* that no one ever questions the Vikings' actions. We will return in due course to the question of the Vikings' actions when we consider the shield wall phase of the battle and the reasons behind Byrhtnoth's decision to allow the Vikings to cross the causeway.

The demand for tribute may well have been genuine. The Vikings had everything to gain and nothing to lose by such a demand. Equally, the English refusal, seen in the light of earlier (rather than later) events – namely the Alfredian success and the subsequent unification of England – will have given the English no pause for doubt in dismissing out of hand the Vikings' request for silver. As for the numbers involved, the Anglo-Saxon Chronicle A manuscript speaks of ninety-three ships; with regard to the English, suffice it to say Byrhtnoth was an experienced soldier and probably possessed the numbers to do the job, particularly as he may have been expecting reinforcements by sea.

Separated still by 'the waters of Pante', both sides engaged in ineffectual sniping, certainly with bows but also probably with javelins. The next low tide was at 5.20 p.m. and once the causeway became clear, or at least crossable, Byrhtnoth seized the initiative. Putting a force onto the causeway, the English effectively blocked the Vikings, trapping them on the island, but as will be seen, it was a trap with no jaws. Wulfstan and his two companions, Ælfhere and Maccus, were in a strong position. Their flanks were secure, for the mud on either side of the causeway is deep and clinging, making movement through it, in military terms, impossible. Even if the Vikings attempted to wade through the mud, and we have no evidence or reason to suppose that they did, then they would have found the crossing slow, exhausting and disruptive to any formation, and they would have arrived at the English-held bank exhausted and piecemeal and would have died exhausted and piecemeal. The causeway was the only way across yet it was easily blocked by a small force; neither side could properly engage the other – a state of impasse had been reached.

> They [the Vikings] asked to be allowed to have passage
> to cross over the ford, to advance their troops
>
> *The Battle of Maldon*, lines 87–88

Then Byrhtnoth, because of his *ofermod*, his over-weaning pride, his over-confidence, pulled back his forces and allowed the Vikings passage of the causeway. Now we come to reasons, to ask why, why did Byrhtnoth allow the Vikings to cross? And why did the Vikings seek battle?

Byrhtnoth's motives are the easiest to fathom. He had done the impossible – he had intercepted the force that had ravaged Folkestone, Sandwich and Ipswich before they attacked their next target; however, his triumph was hollow for he could not bring them to battle. Only by defeating them in battle and destroying their forces could Byrhtnoth end the raids, not only now but also potentially in the future, by sending a message that England, or at least this part of England, was well-defended and that similar adventures would end the way, namely in the death and defeat of the raiders. Byrhtnoth therefore had little choice; if he was to fight the battle he had planned to fight, the Vikings had to be allowed to cross to the mainland. Byrhtnoth's decision therefore had nothing to do with *ofermod*; instead, it had everything to do with the reality of the situation facing him. As for *ofermod*, despite Tolkien's damning inditement of it, in an aristocratic warrior milieu was it not rather a virtue, as opposed to the fault it is usually portrayed as? Were not all the great figures of Anglo-Saxon literature and history, Beowulf, Finn, Edgar with his second imperial coronation at Bath, even Alfred when his piety allowed it, not to some extent guilty of *ofermod*? Pride, arrogance, swagger were possessed by all of the great commanders of history. These character traits, which in civilian life are seen as unappealing, are in military life viewed at times as something akin to virtues – particularly, as was the case in Anglo-Saxon England, in an age of heroic leadership. They are a way a leader exudes confidence both in himself and his men; they are morale building and boosting and morale wins battle.

What then of the Vikings? The Vikings were conducting a campaign of raiding and pitched battles were not, so to speak, on their 'to-do' list; indeed, they were to be avoided at all costs. Why then did they seek to cross the causeway?

The Vikings were faced with a number of problems, and in military intelligence terms they could not see over the hill – they were merely in a position to guess what was on the other side of it. As Pullen-Appleby pointed out in his 2005 study *English Sea Power*, the Anglo-Saxons' preferred tactic for dealing with a raiding force such as the one currently languishing on Northey Island was to pin it between a land and a naval force. The Vikings undoubtedly knew this and may well have been expecting English warships to make an appearance as soon as conditions, namely the tide, were favourable. The non-appearance at this stage presented the Vikings with an opportunity to defeat the force in front of them before having to deal with any new threat, if and/or when it should appear. It would be better to fight concurrent battles than to face two enemy forces from different directions. Of course, we do not know if Byrhtnoth was expecting naval support. Maybe he was and it had failed to appear, maybe he knew it would not arrive in time to help decide the issue, or maybe there was none available. Whatever the case, upper-most in the mind of each of the commanders was the question of escape. Byrhtnoth could not afford to let the Vikings escape, as he could not be certain that he would ever bring them to battle again. As for the Vikings, I believe that they did not see escape without battle as an option, and if they were going to have to fight, then now was the best time, for the longer they sat there the likelier it was that the forces arrayed against them, both on land and also possibly at sea, would increase to such a point as to make victory and thus any chance of escape impracticable.

Crossing the causeway,

> the sailors carried their lime-wood shields on to the land.
> There again the fierce ones stood ready
> Byrhtnoth with his men. He commanded that with the shields

They form the shieldwall, and that the company hold out
Firm against the fiends. Then the fight was near

Battle of Maldon, lines 99–103

At this point a further exchange of missiles occurred, and then the two sides closed to contact.

The dynamics of shield wall combat have already been considered and discussed at some length earlier in this work. Therefore, rather than go over the issues and reiterate the evidence, we shall instead examine the event that broke the symmetry of the shield wall and decisively settled the combat – namely the death of Byrhtnoth.

How soon it occurred after the shield walls collided is impossible to say. Heroic leadership and the death in battle of a leader need not, given the correct set of circumstances, prove fatal to a side's chances of winning, although the mere belief that William was dead very nearly proved disastrous for the Norman cause at Hastings. However, hindsight has in a way distorted our view of the events of that day in August, with Byrhtnoth's *ofermod* being blamed for the English defeat. Yet to view events in this light would be wrong, for up until his death, everything, as far as Byrhtnoth was concerned, seemed to be going right; his strategy, such as we can glean of it, was working, albeit with a little luck. Byrhtnoth was lucky to have intercepted the Vikings before they sacked Maldon; his luck held in that he was able, despite the problems of the terrain, to bring them to battle. His luck failed, or rather luck turned and favoured the Vikings, in the bloody constraint of battle.

Then did the lack-willed leave the battlefield

The Battle of Maldon, line 185

While Byrhtnoth's death provided the catalyst for the English defeat, it was ironically the belief that he was alive that broke the shield wall and led the better part of the *fyrd* into flight.

Byrhtnoth died fighting in the centre of the English line, with his household around him. Then, like a scene taken straight out of the *Iliad*, a fight developed over his body and his armour, in the course of which both Ælfnoth and Wulfmær, who stood beside their lord, were also slain (*The Battle of Maldon*, lines 182–183). Even in the middle of this Homeric contest the English cause was not necessarily lost, for by its very nature close-order infantry combat shielded the ealdorman's death from the majority of his men. Yet here, in this death, we see one of the flaws of heroic leadership. For those who saw it, there was an immediate effect on morale. For some, and we will return to this point in a moment, it spurred them, so the poet would have us believe, on to great deeds. On others it had quite the opposite effect.

'If the best of us is dead what chance have we lesser mortals' may well sum up the attitude of those who 'departed from the battlefield' (*The Battle of Maldon*, line 185).

The trickling of men away from fighting, if the process began in this fashion, and line 185 of the poem appears to have implied that it did, would certainly not have gone unnoticed by the rest of the English line, and it practically goes without saying that the effect would have been unsettling. The trickle turned into a flood when 'Godric quit the field' (*The Battle of Maldon*, line 187), for in his haste to escape he took Byrhtnoth's horse. This fateful horse was undoubtedly not only the best mount present, but was also, importantly, the most recognisable. Thus it was the belief that Byrhtnoth was alive, possibly wounded, but definitely alive, and fleeing the field that brought ruin to the English cause that day. Not, ironically, his death. Indeed it is possible, had all Byrhtnoth's household (and Godric and his brothers were a part of the household) proved loyal, that the English may yet have prevailed and won the day. But it was not to be.

It appears that the flanks of Anglo-Saxon host disintegrated, leaving the remains (those who were neither dead nor fled) of the centre, the household troop, still engaged with the enemy. From this point on (line 202), the poem deals with the fate of the individual members of Byrhtnoth's *comitatus*. On a purely practical level, it must be remembered that disengagement and retirement in the face of the enemy is one of the hardest tricks to pull off. The centre of the English line was probably the most heavily engaged; it may have been driving the Vikings back, and in such circumstances disengagement may have been impossible. In this case, the final part of the poem may be viewed simply as a case of putting a heroic gloss over the military realities of the situation.

Less cynically, Byrhtnoth's *comitatus* were probably not in any position to disengage from the Vikings. Equally, they were not cowards, and while they undoubtedly had a realistic view of their situation, they were also the product of their society. Their background, training, and upbringing were aristocratic, heroic and martial. Given the situation, they could do nothing less than to fight and die to avenge their lord. Indeed, their very education had taught them that this was, in these circumstances, both right and proper.

To the victors – escape. The price of victory was, it appears, too high for anything else. Sunset was at 7.19 p.m. and the taking of a prepared and defended Maldon at night, even one shocked by the English defeat (the defenders may not as yet have been aware of the death of Byrhtnoth), was it appears beyond the Vikings' reach. There is nothing bloodier than two western armies facing each other in battle. We lack casualty figures for the engagement, but it may be, indeed it appears likely, that the English force, particularly the last stand of Byrhtnoth's household, exacted a heavy toll before they themselves were destroyed. The fact that Maldon itself escaped sack shows that Byrhtnoth at least succeeded in one respect.

However, the preservation of Maldon and the possibility of heavy Viking casualties cannot detract from the fact that this was anything other than a defeat for the English, a defeat made all the worse by the death of one of the country's leading men. The failure to use naval forces to interdict the now weakened raiders, combined with the 'buying of peace' and the departure of the Vikings, merely served to compound the extent of the defeat.

The final battles of the Viking Age were not quite the same as the earlier engagements and the reason for this lies back in the events of AD 1013. Up to this point, even though at times quite large forces had been involved, particularly in the conquest period, they remained raiding-armies: disparate forces, collections of boat crews brought together under, generally, a number of leaders, where the sole purpose was the accumulation of wealth, even if that wealth came latterly in the form of land.

Swein of Denmark's invasion in AD 1013 changed all of that. Prior to this point, the forces of the state had been involved in defending the state by land and by sea from piratical raiders. Now, however, we see the forces of one sovereign state ranged against the forces of another sovereign state. We see a return to the *kabinetskrieg* that characterised the wars between the Anglo-Saxon kingdoms. However, whereas the wars of the Heptarchy could by seen as hegemonic wars, the same cannot be said of the wars of Swein Forkbeard and his successor. The campaigns waged by Swein, and his son Cnut, were aimed at conquest.

The battles of AD 1013–16 are poorly described. What they did achieve, with the premature death of Edmund Ironside and the accession of Cnut to the throne of the whole of England, was the creation of an Anglo-Danish military structure and kingdom. This was in many ways the great triumph of the Vikings and the end of an age.

Turning briefly to the events of AD 1066, on the battlefield at least, we see the clash of three, if not pure Viking, then Viking-descended armies. The Norwegian and Anglo-Danish forces had remained closest to their roots and while this may be seen as an argument for why the Normans won, let us not forget that the final battle (Hastings) was one of the most closely fought of any age. The length and closeness of Hastings shows that the Viking/Anglo-Saxon way of war – the reliance on close-order heavy infantry – while not wholly bankrupt was no longer wholly sufficient for the needs of what was then modern warfare. This view was further reinforced at Dyrrachion in AD 1081. Here the Varangians, despite standing up to and helping to defeat the initial Norman attack, suffered heavy casualties when they became separated from the rest of the Byzantine army. However, as the battles of Tinchebrai in AD 1106, Bremule in AD 1119 and Bourgtherolde in AD 1124 show, for Anglo-Norman royal armies the dismounting of knights to form a body of heavy infantry was, when combined with archery and mounted knights, a battle winning combination. Thus, Anglo-Viking tactics did not completely disappear as a result of the events of AD 1066.

Bibliography

Abels, R. P., 1988: *Lordship and Military Obligation in Anglo-Saxon England*, London.

Abels, R. P. and Bachrach, B. S. (eds.), 2001: *The Normans and Their Adversaries at War: Essays in Memory of C. Warren Hollister*, Woodbridge.

Aitchison, N., 2003: *The Picts and the Scots at War*, Stroud.

Arnold, T., 2001: *The Renaissance at War*, London.

Bachrach, B. S., 2001: *Early Carolingian Warfare: Prelude to Empire*, Philadelphia.

Backhouse, J., Turner, D. H. and Webster, L., 1984: *The Golden Age of Anglo-Saxon Art 966–1066*, London.

Bailey, R. N., 1980: *Viking Age Sculpture in Northern England*, London.

Barlow, F., 1970: *Edward the Confessor*, London.

Barlow, F., 2002: *The Godwins*, Harlow.

Bennett, M., 2001: *Campaigns of the Norman Conquest*, Oxford.

Bradbury, J., 1985: *The Medieval Archer*, Woodbridge.

Bradbury, J., 1998: *The Battle of Hastings*, Stroud.

Brøgger, A. W. and Shetelig, H., 1951: *The Viking Ships: Their Ancestry and Evolution*, Oslo.

Brooks, N., 2000: *Communities and Warfare 700–1400*, London.

Cameron, E. A., 2000: *Sheaths and Scabbards in England AD 400–1100*, Oxford.

Christensen, A. E. (ed.), 1996: *The Earliest Ships: The Evolution of Boats into Ships*, London.

Christiansen, E., 2002: *The Norsemen in the Viking Age*, Oxford.

Cooper, J. (ed.), 1993: *The Battle of Maldon: Fiction and Fact*, London.

Crumlin-Pedersen, O., 1997: *Viking-Age Ships and Shipbuilding in Hedeby/ Haithabu and Schleswig*, Roskilde.

Crumlin-Pedersen, O., 2010: *Archaeology and the Sea in Scandinavia and Britain: A Personal Account*, Roskilde.

Davidson, H. R. E., 1962: *The Sword in Anglo-Saxon England: Its Archaeology and Literature*, Woodbridge.

Davies, S., 2004: *Welsh Military Institutions 633–1283*, Cardiff.

DeVries, K., 1999: *The Norwegian Invasion of England in 1066*, Woodbridge.

Dickinson, T. and Härke, H., 1992: *Early Anglo-Saxon Shields*, London.

Downham, C., 2007: *Viking Kings of Britain and Ireland: The Dynasty of Ívarr to A.D. 1014*, Edinburgh.

Durham, K., 2002: *Viking Longship*, Oxford.

Evans, S. S., 1997: *The Lords of Battle: Image and Reality of the* Comitatus *in Dark-Age Britain*, Woodbridge.

Falk, H., 1914: *Altnordische Waffenkunde*, Kristiania.

Ferguson, R., 2009: *The Hammer and the Cross: A New History of the Vikings*, London.

Fett, P., 1938/39: *Arms in Norway: between 400 and 600 A.D.*, Bergen.

Fletcher, I. (ed.), 1998: *The Peninsular War: Aspects of the Struggle for the Iberian Peninsular*, Staplehurst.

Foote, P. and Wilson, D. M., 1970: *The Viking Achievement: The Society and Culture of Early Medieval Scandinavia*, London.

Forte, A., Oram, R. and Pedersen, F., 2005: *Viking Empires*, Cambridge.

France, J., 1994: *Victory in the East: A Military History of the First Crusade*, Cambridge.

France, J., 1999: *Western Warfare in the Age of the Crusades 1000-1300*, London.

France, J. and DeVries, K. (eds.), 2008: *Warfare in the Dark Ages*, Aldershot.

Gaebel, R. E., 2002: *Cavalry Operations in the Ancient Greek World*, Norman.

Goldsworthy, A. K., 1996: *The Roman Army at War 100BC–AD200*, Oxford.

Gräslund, A-S., 1981: *Birka IV. The Burial Customs: A study of the graves on Björkö*, Stockholm.

Gravett, C., 1992: *Hastings 1066: The Fall of Saxon England*, Oxford.

Gravett, C., 1993: *Norman Knight 950–1204AD*, London.

Grieg, S., 1947: *Gjermundbufunnet*, Oslo.

Griffith, P., 1995: *The Viking Art of War*, London.

Haldon, J., 2001: *The Byzantine Wars: Battles and Campaigns of the Byzantine Era*, Stroud.

Halsall, G., 2003: *Warfare and Society in the Barbarian West, 450–900*, London.

Hanson, V. D., 1990: *The Western Way of War: Infantry Battle in Classical Greece*, Oxford.

Hanson, V. D. (ed.), 1991: *Hoplites: The Classical Greek Battle Experience*, London.

Hardy, R., 1976: *The Longbow: A Social and Military History*, Sparkford.

Harris, V., 2004: *Cutting Edge: Japanese Swords in the British Museum*, London.

Harrison, M., 1993: *Viking Hersir 793–1066AD*, London.

Hawkes, S. C. (ed.), 1989: *Weapons and Warfare in Anglo-Saxon England*, Oxford.

Hedenstierna-Jonson, C. and Olausson, L. H., 2006: *The Oriental Mounts from Birka's Garrison: An Expression of Warrior Rank and Status*, Stockholm.

Higham, N. J., 1997: *The Death of Anglo-Saxon England*, Stroud.

Hill, D. and Rumble, A. R. (eds.), 1996: *The Defence of Wessex: The Burghal Hidage and Anglo-Saxon Fortifications*, Manchester.

Hollister, C. W., 1962: *Anglo-Saxon Military Institutions on the Eve of the Norman Conquest*, Oxford.

Howard, I., 2003: *Swein Forkbeard's Invasion and the Danish Conquest of England, 991–1017*, Woodbridge.

Howarth, D., 1968: *Waterloo: A Near Run Thing*, Glasgow.

Howarth, D., 1977: *1066: The Year of the Conquest*.

Jesch, J., 2001: *Ships and Men in the Late Viking Age: The Vocabulary of Runic Inscriptions and Skaldic Verse*, Woodbridge.

John, E., 1964: *Land Tenure in Early England: A Discussion of Some Problems*, Leicester.

John, E., 1966: *Orbis Britanniae and Other Studies*, Leicester.

John, E., 1996: *Reassessing Anglo-Saxon England*, Manchester.

Jones, C., 2006: *The Forgotten Battle of 1066 Fulford*, Stroud.

Jørgensen, A. N. and Clausen, B. L., 1997: *Military Aspects of Scandinavian Society in a European Perspective, AD1–1300*, Copenhagen.

Jørgensen, A. N., Pind, J., Jørgensen, L. and Clausen, B. (eds.), 2002: *Maritime Warfare in Northern Europe: Technology, Organisation, Logistics and Administration 500BC–1500AD*, Copenhagen.

Jörgensen, C. (et al.), 2005: *Fighting Techniques of the Early Modern World AD1500–AD1763: Equipment, Combat Skills and Tactics*, Staplehurst.

Kagay, D. J. and Villalon, L. J. A. (eds.), 1999: *The Circle of War in the Middle Ages: Essays on Medieval Military and Naval History*, Woodbridge.

Kendrick, T. D., 1949: *Late Saxon and Viking Art*, London.

Lavelle, R., 2002: *Æthelred II: King of the English 978–1016*, Stroud.

Lavelle, R., 2003: *Fortifications in Wessex c.800–1066*, Oxford.

Lavelle, R., 2010: *Alfred's Wars: Sources and Interpretations of Anglo-Saxon Warfare in the Viking Age*, Woodbridge.

Lawson, M. K., 1993: *Cnut: The Danes in England in the Early Eleventh Century*, London.

Lawson, M. K., 2002: *The Battle of Hastings 1066*, Stroud.

Lendon, J. E., 2005: *Soldiers & Ghosts: A History of Battle in Classical Antiquity*, New Haven.

Leppäaho, J., 1964: *Späteisenzeitliche Waffen aus Finnland*, Helsinki.

Lindholm, D. and Nicolle, D., 2003: *Medieval Scandinavian Armies (1) 1100–1300*, Oxford.

Lindholm, D. and Nicolle, D., 2007: *The Scandinavian Baltic Crusades 1100–1500*, Oxford.

Loyn, H. R., 1977: *The Vikings in Britain*, London.

McGeer, E., 1995: *Sowing the Dragon's Teeth: Byzantine Warfare in the Tenth Century*, Washington D.C.

McGlynn, S., 2008: *By Sword and Fire: Cruelty and Atrocity in Medieval Warfare*, London.

Morillo, S., 1994: *Warfare under the Anglo-Norman Kings 1066–1135*, Woodbridge.

Morillo, S., (ed.) 1996: *The Battle of Hastings: Sources and Interpretations*, Woodbridge.

Nafziger, G., 1996: *Imperial Bayonets: Tactics of the Napoleonic Battery, Battalion and Brigade as Found in Contemporary Regulations*, London.

Nicolle, D., 1984: *Arthur and the Anglo-Saxon Wars*, London.

Nicolle, D., 1999: *Arms and Armour of the Crusading Era 1050–1350* (2 vols.), Woodbridge.

Nicolle, D., 1999: *Armies of Medieval Russia 750–1250*, Oxford.

Nicolle, D., 2005: *Carolingian Cavalryman AD768–987*, Oxford.

Nicolle, D., 2008: *Poitiers AD732: Charles Martel turns the Islamic tide*, Oxford.

Oakeshott, E., 1960: *The Archaeology of Weapons: Arms and Armour from Prehistory to the Age of Chivalry*, London.

Oakeshott, E., 1994: *The Sword in the Age of Chivalry*, Woodbridge.

Olsen, O. and Crumlin-Pedersen, O., 1978: *Five Viking Ships from Roskilde Fjord*, Copenhagen.

Oman, C., 1924: *A History of the Art of War in the Middle Ages 378–1485AD* (2 vols.), London.

Owen-Crocker, G. R., (ed.) 2005: *King Harold II and the Bayeux Tapestry*, Woodbridge.

Petersen, J., 1919: *Die Norske Vikingesverd*, Kristiania.

Peirce, I., 2002: *Swords of the Viking Age*, Woodbridge.

Poole, R. G., 1991: *Viking Poems on War and Peace: A Study in Skaldic Narrative*, Toronto.

Powicke, M., 1962: *Military Obligation in Medieval England*, Oxford.

Price, N. S., 2002: *The Viking Way: Religion and War in Late Iron Age Scandinavia*, Uppsala.

Pullen-Appleby, J., 2005: *English Sea Power c871 to 1100*, Hockwold-cum-Wilton.

Richards, J., 2002: *Landsknecht Soldier 1486–1560*, Oxford.

Riché, P., 1978: *Daily Life in the World of Charlemagne*, Liverpool.

Robinson, J., 2004: *The Lewis Chessmen*, London.

Rodger, N. A. M., 1997: *The Safeguard of the Sea: A Naval History of Britain Volume One 660–1649*, London.

Roesdahl, E., 1982: *Viking Age Denmark*, London.

Roesdahl, E., 1991: *The Vikings*, London.

Roesdahl, E. and Wilson, D. M. (eds.), 1992: *From Viking to Crusader: The Scandinavians and Europe 800–1200*, Council of Europe.

Rose, S., 2002: *Medieval Naval Warfare 1000–1500*, London.

Salmo, H., 1938: *Die Waffen der Merowingerzeit in Finland*, Helsinki.

Sawyer, P. (ed.), 1997: *The Oxford Illustrated History of the Vikings*, Oxford.

Scragg, D. (ed.), 1991: *The Battle of Maldon AD991*, Oxford.

Shetelig, H., Falk, H. and Gordon, E. V., 1937: *Scandinavian Archaeology*, Oxford.

Shetelig, H. (ed.), 1940: *Viking Antiquities in Great Britain and Ireland* (six volumes), Oslo.

Snodgrass, A. M., 1999: *Arms and Armour of the Greeks*, Baltimore.

Stafford, P., 1989: *Unification and Conquest: A Political and Social History of England in the Tenth and Eleventh Centuries*, London.

Starkey, D., 2004: *The Monarchy of England: The Beginnings*, London.

Stenton, F. (ed.), 1957: *The Bayeux Tapestry: A Comprehensive Survey*, London.

Stephenson, I. P., 1999: *Roman Infantry Equipment: The Later Empire*, Stroud.

Stephenson, I. P., 2002: *The Anglo-Saxon Shield*, Stroud.

Stephenson, I. P., 2006: *Romano-Byzantine Infantry Equipment*, Stroud.

Stephenson, I. P., 2007: *The Late Anglo-Saxon Army*, Stroud.

Strickland, M. (ed.), 1992: *Anglo-Norman Warfare: Studies in Late Anglo-Saxon and Anglo-Norman Military Organization and Warfare*, Woodbridge.

Strickland, M. and Hardy, R., 2005: *The Great Warbow: From Hastings to the Mary Rose*, Stroud.

Swanton, M. J., 1973: *The Spearheads of the Anglo-Saxon Settlements*, London.

Syvänne, I., 2004: *The Age of Hippotoxotai: Art of War in Roman Military Revival and Disaster (491–636)*, Tampere.

Tweddle, D., 1992: *The Anglian Helmet from Coppergate*, York.

Underwood, R., 1999: *Anglo-Saxon Weapons and Warfare*, Stroud.

van Wees, H., 2004: *Greek Warfare: Myths and Realities*, London.

Wallace-Hadrill, J. M., 1975: *Early Medieval History*, Oxford.

Wheeler, R. E. M., 1927: *London and the Vikings*, London.

Whitelock, D., 1952: *The Beginnings of English Society: The Anglo-Saxon Period*, Harmondsworth.

Wilson, D. M., 1984: *Anglo-Saxon Art: from the Seventh Century to the Norman Conquest*, London.

Wilson, D. M., 1985: *The Bayeux Tapestry*, London.

Index

Armour, 40–54
  Body armour, 49–53
    Mail, 51–3
    Lamellar, 53
  Greaves, 53
  Helmets, 41–7
  Shields, 47–9
  Under-armour padding, 53–4
  Vambraces, 53

Battle, 104–13
Battles
  Ashdown, 105
  Brunanburh, 105–6
  Dyrrachion, 113
  Hastings, 113
  Maldon, 107–12
Beowulf, 25, 29, 34, 37, 40, 50, 59,
  67, 69, 77
Berserkirs, 20–3

Capitularies, 71–2
Cavalry, 86–90, 97

Fight at Finnsburg, 40, 50, 81

Heriots, 73–4

Longships, 99
  Gokstad, 14, 23, 46–7, 67, 90
  Ladeby, 67, 90

Oseberg, 14, 23, 67, 90

Naval warfare, 98–101

Raiding, 94–8
  Jarrow, 7, 26–7, 97
  Lindisfarne, 8, 23, 25–6, 94–5, 98

Sagas, 19–20
Shieldwall, 77–86
Siege warfare, 101–4
Sieges
  London, 103–4
  Paris, 103–4
  Reading, 102
  Repton, 102
  York, 104

Weapons, 54–69
  Axe, 59–62
  Bow, 65–9, 90–2
  Crossbow, 69
  Javelins, 69
  Mace, 62–3
  Seax, 56–9
  Solenarion, 69
  Spear, 63–5
  Sword, 55–6
    Scabbards, 55–6
    Sword suspension, 56
  Wedge, 79–80